Study Guide

to accompany

Essentials
of
Economics

Study Guide

to accompany

Essentials
of
Economics

Third Edition

Bradley R. Schiller
American University

Prepared by
Linda Wilson
University of Texas, Arlington

Thomas Anderson
Montgomery College

Boston   Burr Ridge, IL   Dubuque, IA   Madison, WI   New York   San Francisco   St. Louis
Bangkok   Bogotá   Caracas   Lisbon   London   Madrid
Mexico City   Milan   New Delhi   Seoul   Singapore   Sydney   Taipei   Toronto

Irwin/McGraw-Hill

A Division of The McGraw·Hill Companies

Study Guide to accompany
ESSENTIALS OF ECONOMICS

3 4 5 6 7 8 9 0 QPD/QPD 3 2 1 0

ISBN 0-07-303273-5

http://www.mhhe.com

Table of Contents

Preface

This study guide is written to accompany *Essentials of Economics*, 3rd edition, by Bradley R. Schiller. The overall focus of the study guide is reinforce the economic principles and concepts presented in the textbook. Each section of each chapter has a particular objective.

The *Quick Review* and *Learning Objectives* sections provide brief summaries of the basic contents of the corresponding text chapters.

The *Using Key Terms* section allows students to practice using the words defined in each chapter in a crossword puzzle format.

The *True or False* and *Multiple Choice* sections help students to apply economic principles in a familiar problem-solving setting. This will help greatly in the preparation for exams.

The *Problems and Applications* section lets students discover economic principles for themselves. Students not only learn the techniques that economists use, but they also discover the basis for the economic concepts they have learned.

Semester after semester, students have difficulty with the same concepts and make the same mistakes. The section called *Common Errors* addresses some of these areas, and provides an explanation using appropriate economic principles.

STUDY GUIDE
Acknowledgments

We thank the McGraw-Hill staff for their support. Paul Shensa is a wonderful editor. Kezia Pearlman, developmental editor, is a real professional. We thank her for her willingness to help and for her skillful management of the project. We also thank Lance Griggs and Anthony Mendez for providing the graphics for this edition.

Linda L. Wilson
The University of Texas at Arlington

Thomas Anderson
Montgomery College, Maryland

CHAPTER 1

The Challenge of Economics

Quick Review

- The resources—land, labor, capital, and entrepreneurship—available to any economy measure its ability to satisfy society's desires for goods and services.

- Every society confronts the problem of scarcity because the desire for goods and services exceeds the economy's resources, which are used to produce the goods and services.

- Because of scarcity, every economy must answer three basic questions: WHAT is to be produced? HOW is it to be produced? and FOR WHOM is it to be produced?

- The WHAT question involves finding and producing the optimal (or best) mix of output.

- The production-possibilities curve demonstrates the limits of society's ability to produce at any point in time given its resources and technology. All production entails opportunity costs because the resources used to produce one thing cannot be used simultaneously to produce something else.

- Additional resources and technological advances result in an outward shift in the production-possibilities curve or economic growth.

- The responsibility for answering the WHAT, HOW, and FOR WHOM questions is jointly shared by government and the market.

- The market mechanism allocates resources by relying on sales and changes in relative prices to signal the goods and services society desires.

- Most economies are "mixed" because neither the market mechanism nor government alone can lead to the optimal mix of output. Market failure occurs when the market mechanism leads society to an output mix other than the optimal level; government failure occurs when intervention does not improve the outcome.

- The HOW question is focused on society's choice among techniques for producing various goods and services. Government frequently intervenes in ways that favor certain techniques.

- The FOR WHOM question involves the distribution of output. Again there is a role for markets and a role for government as it levies taxes and makes transfers.

- Microeconomics is concerned with the behavior of households, firms, and government agencies; macroeconomics with economywide issues and goals.

1

Learning Objectives

After studying the chapter and doing the following exercises you should:

1. Understand why scarcity is a problem faced by all societies.
2. Be able to describe the WHAT, HOW, and FOR WHOM questions.
3. Be able to demonstrate the idea of opportunity cost using a production-possibilities curve.
4. Understand the concept of economic growth.
5. Be able to explain the concept of the market mechanism.
6. Understand why most economies are "mixed economies."
7. Be able to articulate the historical relationship between political and economic forces.
8. Know the difference between market failure and government failure and why each occurs.
9. Know the difference between macroeconomics and microeconomics.

Using Key Terms

Fill in the puzzle on the opposite page with the appropriate term from the list of Terms to Remember on page 25 in the text.

Across

1. The tradeoff experienced by choosing to watch TV instead of reading your text book.
3. A likely result of government intervention according to the survey on page 20 in the text.
5. Represented by land, labor, capital, and entrepreneurship.
6. Economic study concerned with the behavior of individuals, firms, and government agencies.
9. Expenditure on new plant and equipment, for example.
13. Referred to as the "invisible hand" by Adam Smith.
14. Latin term meaning "other things remaining equal."
15. Economic policy supported by Adam Smith.

Down

2. The curve represented in Figure 1.1 in the text.
4. The study of the economy as a whole.
7. The use of both market signals and government directives to select the mix of output.
8. Illustrated in Figure 1.6 in the text by the outward shift of the production-possibilities curve.
10. The study of how best to allocate society's scarce resources.
11. Represented by point M in Figure 1.7 in the text.
12. The central economic problem addressed in the article, "Americans Have It All," on page 4 in the text.

Puzzle 1.1

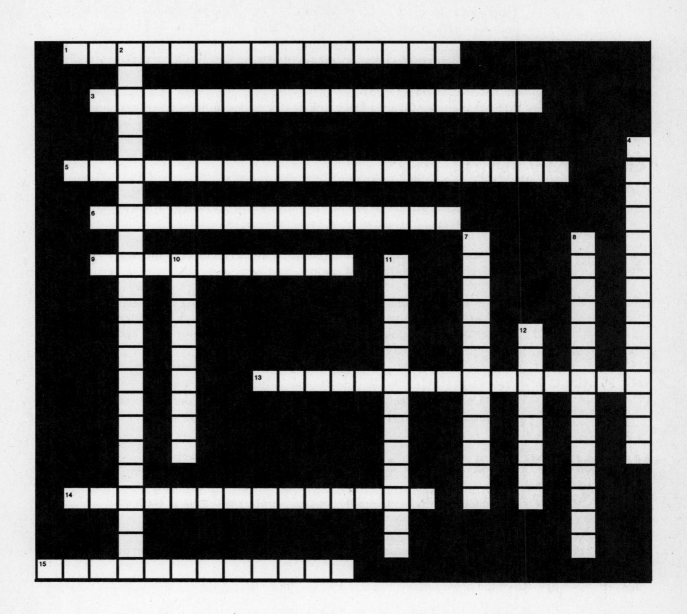

True or False: *Circle your choice and explain why any false statements are incorrect.*

T   F   1.   The United States is a prosperous nation because its resources are sufficient to meet the desires of its citizens.

T   F   2.   Resources are scarce because our desire for goods and services exceeds the ability of our resources to produce goods and services.

T   F   3.   A production-possibilities curve demonstrates graphically the concept of virtually unlimited human desires for goods and services.

T   F   4.   The proportion of United States output allocated to military goods has remained relatively constant since World War II.

T   F   5.   The opportunity cost of a good is the sacrifice of all the alternative goods that are forgone.

T   F   6.   To experience greater economic growth, an economy must sacrifice present consumption.

T   F   7.   The best answer to the HOW to produce question for an economy is the method of production that uses the most labor.

T   F   8.   Adam Smith encouraged a policy of "laissez faire" because he believed that the market mechanism provided society with the best answers to the WHAT, HOW, and FOR WHOM questions.

T   F   9.   Market failure is always corrected by government intervention.

T   F   10.   The United States economy is referred to as a planned economy because a large proportion of our resources are allocated by the government.

Multiple Choice: *Select the correct answer.*

____D____   1. The U.S. is capable of producing more goods and services now than in 1900 because of:
  (a)   A greater quantity of labor.
  (b)   A greater quantity of capital.
  (c)   Better production technology.
  (d)   All of the above.

____C____   2. Which of the following is *not* a factor of production?
  (a)   A calculator.
  (b)   A worker on an assembly line.
  (c)   The $500,000 it takes to start a new company.
  (d)   A vacant lot in New York City.

4

_B_

3. The economic problem of scarcity exists because:
   (a) We are capable of producing more than people actually want.
   (b) Society's desires exceed the capability of the resources available to satisfy those desires.
   (c) Of opportunity costs.
   (d) The world is running out of resources, such as petroleum for example.

_D_

4. Which of the following are considered to be scarce in the U.S. economy?
   (a) Farmland.
   (b) Machinery.
   (c) Workers.
   (d) All of the above.

_A_

5. I plan on going to a $5 movie this evening instead of studying for an exam. The total opportunity cost of the movie:
   (a) Is what I could have purchased with the $5 plus the study time I forgo.
   (b) Is $5.
   (c) Depends on how good the movie is.
   (d) Is the forgone studying I could have done during the same time.

_B_

6. The opportunity cost of installing a traffic light at a dangerous intersection is:
   (a) Negative, since it will reduce the number of accidents.
   (b) The best possible alternative bundle of other goods or services that must be forgone in order to build and install the traffic light.
   (c) The time lost by drivers who approach the intersection when the light is red.
   (d) The cost of the stoplight plus the cost savings from a reduction in the number of accidents.

_C_

7. The market mechanism:
   (a) Works through central planning by the government.
   (b) Eliminates market failures created by the government.
   (c) Uses prices as a means of communication between consumers and producers.
   (d) Is not very efficient because there is no direct means of communication between consumers and producers.

_A_

8. Societies must address the question of WHAT to produce because:
   (a) We can't produce all the goods and services we want.
   (b) The amount of money in an economy is limited.
   (c) Of the production-possibilities curve.
   (d) Of market failure.

_b_

9. A point lying inside the production-possibilities curve indicates that:
   (a) There are not enough resources available to reach the production-possibilities curve.
   (b) More output could be produced with existing resources.
   (c) Production is being limited by the level of technology.
   (d) All of the above.

_C_

10. The best answer to the HOW to produce question is the production method that:
    (a) Uses the most labor.
    (b) Maximizes the quantity of all resources used.
    (c) Results in a combination of goods and services on the production-possibilities curve.
    (d) Results in a combination of goods and services outside the production-possibilities curve.

5

_A_ 11. United States welfare programs are an example of:
    (a) How the U.S. has answered the FOR WHOM to produce question.
    (b) Market failure.
    (c) Laissez-faire economics.
    (d) Scarcity.

_B_ 12. If the individuals in an economy wanted to produce a combination of goods and services outside the production-possibilities curve, they would have to:
    (a) Use the best existing technology.
    (b) Find more resources, for example, for such a combination to be possible.
    (c) Use government intervention to command producers to produce more.
    (d) They will never be able to produce a combination of goods and services outside their current production-possibilities curve.

_D_ 13. The sacrifice that typically must be made when an economy increases its rate of growth (i.e. shifts its production-possibilities curve outward) is a tradeoff between:
    (a) Investment and government intervention.
    (b) Unemployment and inflation.
    (c) A market economy and a mixed economy.
    (d) Consumption and investment.

_D_ 14. Government intervention in the economy as a result of market failure will:
    (a) Improve the mix of output produced.
    (b) Worsen the mix of output produced.
    (c) Decrease total output.
    (d) Any of the above could occur.

_C_ 15. Which of the following can be used to correct market failure?
    (a) The market mechanism.
    (b) Laissez-faire price policies.
    (c) Laws and regulations.
    (d) All of the above.

_A_ 16. The collapse of communism is evidence of:
    (a) Government failure.
    (b) Market failure.
    (c) Scarcity.
    (d) *Ceteris paribus.*

_B_ 17. In Figure 1.8 in the text, which of the following combinations of military goods and consumer goods would indicate unused resources?
    (a) Point M.
    (b) Point G_2.
    (c) Points G_1 and G_2.
    (d) Points M, G_1, and G_2.

_A_ 18. The task of economic theory is to:
    (a) Explain and predict economic behavior.
    (b) Make simplifying assumptions.
    (c) Correct market failure.
    (d) Measure opportunity costs.

_C_ 19. The study of economics focuses on:
   (a) The behavior of successful business firms.
   (b) The role of money in our economy.
   (c) How best to allocate scarce resources.
   (d) The elimination of opportunity costs.

_D_ 20. Macroeconomics focuses on the performance of:
   (a) Individual consumers.
   (b) Firms.
   (c) Government agencies.
   (d) The economy as a whole.

Appendix

_B_ 21. If an increase in one variable results in a decrease in the other variable, a graph of the relationship between these two variables would be:
   (a) A straight line.
   (b) A downward sloping line.
   (c) An upward sloping line.
   (d) A line with a slope equal to zero.

_C_ 22. When the relationship between two variables changes:
   (a) There is movement from one point on the curve to another point on the curve.
   (b) The curve is not affected.
   (c) The entire curve shifts.
   (d) The curve becomes linear.

_B_ 23. A linear curve is distinguished by:
   (a) Continuous changes in its slope.
   (b) The same slope throughout the curve.
   (c) The changing relationship between the two variables.
   (d) A shift in the curve.

_C_ 24. The slope of a production-possibilities curve would provide information about:
   (a) The growth of the economy.
   (b) Technological change.
   (c) Opportunity costs.
   (d) Income distribution.

Problems and Applications

Exercise 1

Suppose you have only 20 hours per week to allocate to study or leisure. The following table indicates the tradeoff between leisure time (not studying) and the grade-point average achieved as a result of studying.

Table 1.1

	(a)	(b)	(c)	(d)	(e)
Leisure time (hours / week)	20	18	14.5	9	0
Grade-point average	0	1.0	2.0	3.0	4.0

1. Draw on the graph below the production-possibilities curve that represents the possible combinations from Table 1.1.

Figure 1.1

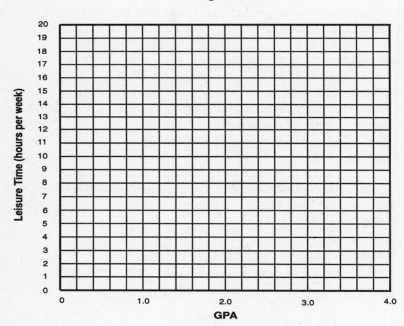

2. Using the information above, what is the opportunity cost of raising your grade-point average from 2.0 to 3.0? _____

3. What is the opportunity cost of raising your grade-point average from 3.0 to 4.0?

   _____

4. Why does the opportunity cost of improving your grade-point average increase?

   _____

8

Exercise 2

This exercise is similar to the problem at the end of Chapter 1 in the text. It provides practice in drawing and interpreting a production-possibilities curve and demonstrating shifts of such a curve.

1. A production-possibilities schedule showing the production alternatives between corn and lumber is presented in Table 1.2. Plot combination *A* in Figure 1.2 and label it. Do the same for combination *B*. In going from combination *A* to combination *B*, the economy has sacrificed _____ billion board feet of lumber production per year and has transferred the land to production of _____ billion bushels of corn per year. The opportunity cost of corn in terms of lumber is _____ board feet per bushel.

Table 1.2

Combination	Quantity of corn (billions of bushels per year)	Quantity of lumber (billions of board feet per year)
A	0	50
B	1	48
C	2	44
D	3	38
E	4	30
F	5	20
G	6	0

2. In answering Question 1 you determined the opportunity cost of corn when the economy is initially producing only lumber (combination *A*). Using the information in Table 1.2, plot the rest of the production-possibilities combinations in Figure 1.2 and label each of the points with the appropriate letter.

Figure 1.2

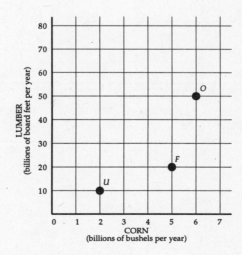

9

3. When Table 1.3 is completed, it should show the opportunity cost of corn at each possible combination of lumber and corn production in the economy. Opposite "1st billion bushels" insert the number of board feet per year of lumber sacrificed when the economy shifts from combination A to combination B. Complete the table for each of the remaining combinations.

Table 1.3

Corn production (billions of bushels per year)	Opportunity cost of corn in terms of lumber (billions of board feet per year)
1st billion bushels	_____
2nd billion bushels	_____
3rd billion bushels	_____
4th billion bushels	_____
5th billion bushels	_____
6th billion bushels	_____

4. In Table 1.3, as more corn is produced (as the economy moves from combination A toward combination G), the opportunity cost of corn _____(falls, rises, remains the same), which illustrates the law of _____.

5. Suppose that lumber companies begin to clear-cut forest areas instead of cutting them selectively. Clear-cutting improves the economy's ability to produce lumber but not corn. Table 1.4 describes such a situation. Using the information in Table 1.4, sketch the new production-possibilities curve in Figure 1.2 as you did the initial production-possibilities curve based on Table 1.3. For which combination does clear-cutting fail to change the amount of corn and lumber produced?

_____

Table 1.4

Combination	Corn (billions of bushels per year)	Lumber (billions of board feet per year)
A'	0	75
B'	1	72
C'	2	66
D'	3	57
E'	4	45
F	5	30
G'	6	0

6. After the introduction of clear-cutting most of the new production-possibilities curve is
    _____ (outside, inside, the same as) the earlier curve. The opportunity cost of corn has
    _____ (increased, decreased) as a result of clear-cutting.

7. Study your original production-possibilities curve in Figure 1.2 and decide which of the combinations shown (*U, F, O*) demonstrates each of the following. (*Hint:* Check the answers at the end of the chapter to make sure you have diagrammed the production-possibilities curve in Figure 1.2 correctly.)

    (a) Society is producing at its maximum potential. Combination_____.
    (b) Society has some unemployed or underemployed resources. Combination _____.
    (c) Society cannot produce this combination. Combination _____.
    (d) Society might be able to produce this combination if technology improved but
         cannot produce it with current technology. Combination _____.
    (e) If society produces this combination, some of society's wants will go unsatisfied
         unnecessarily. Combination _____.

Exercise 3

This exercise requires the use of graphs in conjunction with opportunity cost and production possibilities.

Answer the following questions based on the information on pages 8 through 11 in the text.

_____ 1. The heading "The Choices Nations Make," refers to the tradeoff countries make between:
             (a) Food and consumer goods.
             (b) Consumer goods and military goods.
             (c) Consumption and investment.
             (d) A market economy and a mixed economy.

_____ 2. For the U.S., the share of total output devoted to military goods:
             (a) Has remained fairly constant since 1940.
             (b) Is currently about 25 percent.
             (c) Has decreased since the end of the Cold War.
             (d) Is fairly low and results in no opportunity cost.

_____ 3. According to Figure 1.3 in the text, as the mix of output moves from point *S* to point *R*:
             (a) There is an increase in the production of consumer goods.
             (b) There is no opportunity cost because point *R* represents the optimal mix of output.
             (c) More factors of production are available for both consumer goods and military goods.
             (d) All of the above are true.

_____ 4. According to Figure 1.4 and Figure 1.5 in the text, the North Korean army:
             (a) Is the largest in the world in terms of number of personnel.
             (b) Absorbs over 25 percent of the country's resources.
             (c) Absorbs a smaller share of output than the Chinese army.
             (d) All of the above are true.

5. Which of the following is the opportunity cost of maintaining an army in North Korea?
   (a) There is no opportunity cost because North Korea needs a large army to protect its citizens.
   (b) There is no opportunity cost because North Korea is producing the optimal mix of output.
   (c) Only the money spent on military equipment and salaries.
   (d) The food and other consumer goods that must be given up.

Appendix

Exercise 4

This exercise provides practice in the use of graphs.

Use Figure 1.3 below to answer the following questions.

Figure 1.3

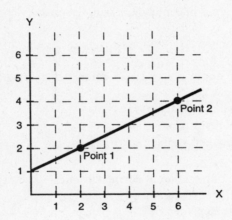

The slope of a line is the rate of change between two points or the vertical change divided by the horizontal change.

1. The vertical distance between the two points equals _____ .

2. The horizontal distance between the two points equals _____ .

3. The slope of the line equals _____ .

4. The slope of the line is (positive, negative) because as one variable increases the other variable (increases, decreases).

5. The line has the same slope at every point implying a (constant, changing) relationship between the two variables.

6. When the slope of a line is the same at every point, the curve is (linear, nonlinear).

Common Errors

The first statement in each "common error" below is incorrect. Each incorrect statement is followed by a corrected version and an explanation.

1. Words used in economics have the same meaning as they do in our everyday conversation. WRONG!
    Words used in everyday conversation *very often* have different meanings when they are used in economics. RIGHT!

    You'll have to be very careful here. Words are used with precision in economics. You'll have difficulty if you confuse their everyday meanings with their economic meanings. For example, the term "capital" in economics refers to goods used in the production of other goods. In everyday usage it may mean money, machines, a loan, or even the British response to the question "How are you feeling?"

2. Economic models are abstractions from the real world and are therefore useless in predicting and explaining economic behavior. WRONG!
    Economic models are abstractions from the real world and *as a result* are useful in predicting and explaining economic behavior. RIGHT!

    You have to be willing to deal with abstractions if you want to get anything accomplished in economics. By using economic models based on specific assumptions, we can make reasonable judgments about what's going on around us. We try not to disregard any useful information. However, to try to include everything (such as what cereal we like for breakfast) would be fruitless. For example, the production-possibilities frontier is an abstraction. No economist would argue that it is an economy! But it certainly is useful in focusing on public-policy choices, such as the choice between guns and butter.

3. Because economics is a "science," all economists should come up with the same answer to any given question. WRONG!
    Economics is a science, but there is often room for disagreement in trying to answer a given question. RIGHT!

    Economics is a social science, and the entire society and economy represent the economist's laboratory. Economists cannot run the kind of experiments on the economy that are done by physical scientists. As a result, two economists may attack a given problem or question in different ways using different models. They may come up with different answers, but since there is no answer book, you cannot say which is right. The solution is, then, to do more testing, refine our models, compare results, and so on. By the way, the recent space probes have given physicists cause to reevaluate much of their theory concerning the solar system, and there is much controversy concerning what the new evidence means. But physics is still a science, as is economics!

■ ANSWERS ■

Using Key Terms

Across

1. opportunity cost
3. government failure
5. factors of production
6. microeconomics
9. investment
13. market mechanism
14. *ceteris paribus*
15. laissez-faire

Down

2. production possibilities
4. macroeconomics
7. mixed economy
8. economic growth
10. economics
11. market failure
12. scarcity

True or False

1. F   Like all societies, the U.S. has to deal with the problem of scarcity. The U.S. is a prosperous nation because it uses its scarce resources efficiently.
2. T
3. F   A production-possibilities curve illustrates graphically the concept that an economy's ability to produce is limited by available resources and technology.
4. F   See Figure 1.2 in the text.
5. F   The opportunity cost of a good is the sacrifice of the next best alternative.
6. T
7. F   The best answer to the HOW to produce question for an economy is the method of production with the lowest opportunity cost.
8. T
9. F   Government intervention may also result in failure.
10. F   The U.S. economy is referred to as a mixed economy because our resources are allocated by both the government and the market.

Multiple Choice

1. d	5. a	9. b	13. d	17. b	21. b
2. c	6. b	10. c	14. d	18. a	22. c
3. b	7. c	11. a	15. c	19. c	23. b
4. d	8. a	12. b	16. a	20. d	24. c

Problems and Applications

Exercise 1

1. **Figure 1.1 Answer**

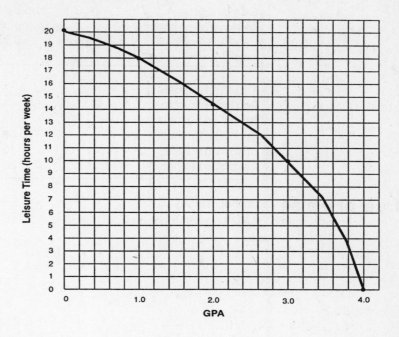

2. 5.5 hours of leisure time.

3. 9 hours of leisure time.

4. Higher grades are harder to get, particularly if the class is graded on a curve, with higher grades being received by a decreasing number of students. Competition is important in the economy and in the classroom.

Exercise 2

1. 2, 1, 2

2. **Figure 1.2 Answer**

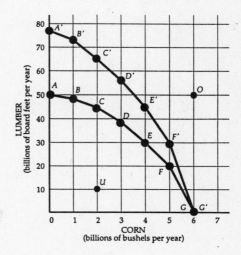

15

3. **Table 1.3 Answer**

Corn production (billions of bushels per year)	Opportunity cost of corn in terms of lumber (billions of board feet per year)
1st billion bushels	2
2nd billion bushels	4
3rd billion bushels	6
4th billion bushels	8
5th billion bushels	10
6th billion bushels	20

4. Rises, increasing opportunity costs
5. See Figure 1.2 answer; combination *G*.
6. Outside, increased
7. a . *F*; b . *U;* c . *O;* d .*O;* e . *U*

Exercise 3

1.	b	3.	a	5.	d
2.	c	4.	b		

Exercise 4

1. 2
2. 4
3. Slope = vertical change/horizontal change = 2/4 = 1/2 or 0.5
4. Positive, increases
5. Constant
6. Linear

CHAPTER 2

The U.S. Economy

Quick Review

- The answers to the WHAT, HOW, and FOR WHOM questions in the U.S. economy are a product of both market activity and government intervention. Economic activity is assessed using economic statistics.

- The most frequently used measure of an economy's production is gross domestic product (GDP), which is the monetary value of a nation's output. Real GDP is the measure of output adjusted for inflation. U.S. GDP, at approximately $8 trillion, is more than one-fifth of the world's total output.

- Per capita GDP for the United States is five times the world's average because abundant resources, skilled management, and an educated work force, combined with advanced technology and other factors, have resulted in high productivity.

- GDP can be classified as consumer goods, investment goods, goods purchased by government—federal, state, and local levels; and net exports. Consumer goods represent the largest portion of U.S. output.

- Over the last century the sector producing the most output in the U. S. has changed from farming, to manufacturing, to services. Service industries now produce over 70 percent of GDP.

- Business organizations take the form of sole proprietorships, partnerships, and corporations; though fewest in number, corporations produce over 90 percent of the nation's output.

- The government frequently regulates HOW output will be produced. Sometimes the answers to the WHAT, HOW, and FOR WHOM questions are made worse by government intervention, which is referred to as "government failure."

- Incomes are distributed quite unequally in the U.S. Those in the highest income quintile receive ten times the income of the average household in the lowest quintile. The tax-and-transfer system redistributes income, which influences the answer to the FOR WHOM question.

Learning Objectives

After studying the chapter and doing the following exercises you should:

1. Understand how the gross domestic product (GDP) is the economy's answer to the WHAT question.
2. Be able to calculate GDP by analyzing the expenditures made by market participants.
3. Be able to identify the expenditures made by households, business, and government sectors.
4. Understand why the answer to the HOW question is shared by markets and government.
5. Understand the historic trends in the industry structure of the U.S. economy.
6. Know the distinguishing characteristics of each form of business organization and its role in the economy.
7. Be able to discuss the FOR WHOM question using the personal distribution of income.
8. Know the impact of the tax-and-transfer system on the answer to the FOR WHOM question.

Using Key Terms

Fill in the puzzle on the opposite page with the appropriate term from the list of Terms to Remember on page 54 in the text.

Across

3. The sum of consumption, investment, government expenditure, and net exports.
4. The resources used to produce goods and services.
9. Goods and services sold to other countries.
11. The knowledge and skills possessed by the labor force.
12. The high level of _____ in the U.S. is explained to some extent by the level of education according to the Headline article on page 45 in the text.
14. The federal income tax system is an example.
15. An expansion of production possibilities.
16. Account for nearly half of all federal government spending but are not part of GDP.
17. A high ratio of capital to labor in the production process.
18. Results in a reverse redistribution of income.

Down

1. Used to compare the standard of living in Table 2.3 in the text.
2. Evaluated in Table 2.4 in the text.
5. Used to compare the size of different economies in Figure 2.1 in the text.
6. Benefits such as public housing and food stamps.
7. A market failure in which the government intervenes to protect consumers from exploitation.
8. Goods and services bought from other countries.
10. The cost or benefit of a market activity that affects a third party.
13. Equals 15 percent of GDP in Figure 2.3 in the text.

Puzzle 2.1

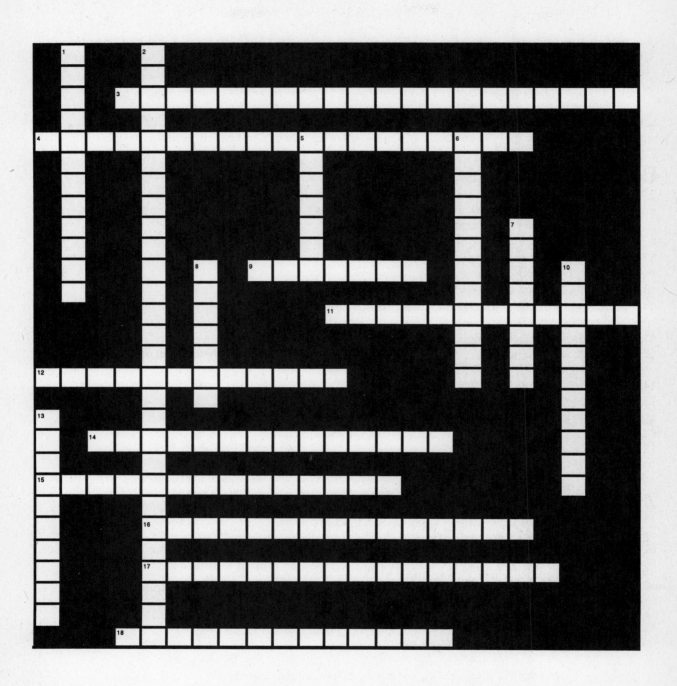

True or False: *Circle your choice and explain why any false statements are incorrect.*

T F 1. GDP only measures the value of goods produced, not services.

T F 2. In periods of rising prices, real GDP will rise more slowly than GDP.

T F 3. Growth in GDP per capita is achieved when population grows more rapidly than GDP.

T F 4. In the U.S., state and local governments use a greater amount of resources than the federal government.

T F 5. If the U.S. consumes more goods and services than it produces, then imports must be greater than exports.

T F 6. Manufacturing output has declined in the U.S. since World War II.

T F 7. The great productivity of the U.S. is the result of using highly educated workers in labor-intensive production processes.

T F 8. Government regulation is necessary when the market fails to use society's scarce resources in the optimal manner.

T F 9. Compared to other countries, the rich in the U.S. have a relatively low share of total income.

T F 10. Taken as a whole, the U.S. tax system is progressive and plays a major role in the redistribution of income.

Multiple Choice: *Select the correct answer.*

 1. The GDP is:
(a) The sum of the physical amounts of goods and services in the economy.
(b) A dollar measure of output produced during a given time period.
(c) A measure of the per capita economic growth rate of the economy.
(d) A physical measure of the capital stock of the economy.

 2. Changes in real GDP serve as a better measure of the health of the economy than GDP because real GDP measures:
(a) Changes in production only.
(b) Changes in prices and production.
(c) Changes in prices only.
(d) Changes in average wages.

 3. In which of the following economies is total output the largest?
(a) Germany.
(b) China.
(c) United States.
(d) Japan.

_D_ 4. If both the prices and the quantities of all final goods and services produced doubled from one year to the next and population remained constant, then:
(a) GDP would be four times as large in the second year as in the first.
(b) Real GDP would be twice as large in the second year as in the first.
(c) On the average, the population could be twice as well off in the second year as in the first.
(d) All of the above would be the case.

_B_ 5. Economic growth involves, *ceteris paribus:*
(a) An increase in imports.
(b) An expansion of production possibilities.
(c) An increase in GDP because of inflation.
(d) An increase in government spending.

_B_ 6. Which of the following groups is the largest user of GDP in the United States?
(a) Federal, state, and local governments.
(b) Private consumers.
(c) Businesses.
(d) Foreigners.

_C_ 7. Which of the following is *not* an example of investment, as economists use the term?
(a) A business builds a new factory.
(b) A private college buys a new lawnmower to replace an old one that has worn out.
(c) A family buys $10,000 worth of stocks.
(d) A department store buys additional men's shirts just before Father's Day.

_A_ 8. Which of the following expenditures is the most important in expanding a country's production possibilities?
(a) Investment goods.
(b) Consumer goods.
(c) Government services.
(d) Net exports.

_D_ 9. Which of the following is *not* included in GDP?
(a) The construction of a highway in Ohio.
(b) The salary of the president of the U.S.
(c) The purchase of West Virginia coal by a Japanese factory.
(d) The payment of disability benefits to a war veteran.

_D_ 10. U.S. net exports are:
(a) Equal to the value of exports minus the value of imports.
(b) Negative if the U.S. imports more than it exports.
(c) Positive if foreigners purchase more U.S. output than the U.S. purchases from foreigners.
(d) All of the above are correct.

_A_ 11. The GDP is larger (smaller) than the sum of U.S. consumption, investment, and government purchases by the amount of U.S.:
(a) Net exports.
(b) Factors of production.
(c) Saving.
(d) Capital stock.

_C_ 12. Which of the following sectors contributes the largest absolute amount to the GDP?
  (a) Farming.
  (b) Manufacturing.
  (c) Services.
  (d) Exports.

_D_ 13. Foreign trade has become increasingly significant to the U.S. economy because of:
  (a) The lowering of trade barriers.
  (b) Improved communication and transportation.
  (c) The growing share of services in the mix of output.
  (d) All of the above are reasons.

_A_ 14. Which of the following would *not* be included in U.S. GDP?
  (a) A computer made by a U.S. firm in Mexico.
  (b) California wine purchased by a French businesswoman.
  (c) A car made by a German producer in South Carolina.
  (d) The meals prepared by a Chinese restaurant in San Francisco.

_D_ 15. Which of the following is a reason why the United States is able to produce such high levels of GDP?
  (a) Abundant factors of production.
  (b) Capital-intensive production.
  (c) High levels of investment in human capital.
  (d) All of the above are reasons.

_A_ 16. Most businesses in the U.S. are classified as:
  (a) Proprietorships.
  (b) Partnerships.
  (c) Corporations.
  (d) Non-profit organizations.

_D_ 17. The government has an impact on the HOW to produce question when it:
  (a) Limits environmental pollution.
  (b) Forbids the use of child labor.
  (c) Sets a minimum wage.
  (d) All of the above are correct.

_B_ 18. If government intervention forces the economy inside the production-possibilities curve, there is:
  (a) Market failure.
  (b) Government failure.
  (c) Externalities.
  (d) Income inequality.

_A_ 19. In the U.S., transfer payments and in-kind benefits represent an attempt to address:
  (a) Income disparity.
  (b) Monopoly power.
  (c) Government failure.
  (d) A regressive tax system.

___C___ 20. Which of the following is the best description of the U.S. tax system?
  (a) The federal income tax is regressive but sales, property, and other taxes tend to be progressive.
  (b) The U.S. tax system is consistently progressive.
  (c) The federal income tax is progressive but sales, property, and other taxes tend to be regressive.
  (d) The U.S. tax system is consistently regressive.

Problems and Applications

Exercise 1

Each January the president has the Council of Economic Advisers prepare an economic report on the state of the U.S. economy called *The Economic Report of the President*. It summarizes the essential features of the economy's performance and describes the policy initiatives that are likely to be undertaken. This exercise uses the kind of information that is developed in this publication.

1. Table 2.1 shows the real GDP and the nominal GDP for the years 1990-97.

Table 2.1. Real GDP and nominal GDP, 1990-97

Year	Real GDP (in billions of dollars per year)	Nominal GDP (in billions of dollars per year)	Percentage growth in real GDP	Percentage growth in nominal GDP	U.S. population (in millions)	Real GDP per capita
1990	6,136.3	5,743.8	--------	--------	249.9	_____
1991	6,079.4	5,916.7	_____	_____	252.6	_____
1992	6,244.4	6,244.4	_____	_____	255.4	_____
1993	6,389.6	6,558.1	_____	_____	258.1	_____
1994	6,610.7	6,947.0	_____	_____	260.6	_____
1995	6,742.1	7,265.4	_____	_____	263.0	_____
1996	6,928.4	7,636.0	_____	_____	265.5	_____
1997	7,191.4	8,083.4	_____	_____	267.9	_____

2.   From the information in Table 2.1, calculate the percentage growth in nominal and real GDP for each of the years 1991-97 and insert your answers in the appropriate columns.
Use the following formula:

$$\text{Percentage growth in real GDP} = \frac{\text{real GDP}_t - \text{real GDP}_{t-1}}{\text{real GDP}_t} \times 100\%$$

where t = current year
    $t - 1$ = previous year

For example, for 1991 real GDP grew by the following percentage:

$$\frac{\text{real GDP}_t - \text{real GDP}_{t-1}}{\text{real GDP}_{t-1}} = \frac{\$6{,}079.4 - \$6{,}136.3}{\$6136.3} \times 100\% = -0.9\%$$

3. T   F   When nominal GDP grows, real GDP must grow.
4. By what nominal-dollar amount did nominal GDP grow from 1990 to 1997? $_____
5. By what constant-dollar amount did real GDP grow from 1990 to 1997? $_____
6. The U.S. population for the years 1990–97 is presented in column 7 of Table 2.1. Calculate the real GDP per capita in column 8.
7. T   F   When real GDP rises, real GDP per capita must also rise.

Exercise 2

This problem is designed to help you learn the way the national-income aggregates are determined and to reinforce your understanding of their relationship to one another.

1. Calculate the percentage of total output accounted for by each of the expenditure categories in Table 2.2. Then compare your answers to Figure 2.3 in the text. Figures will not be exact due to rounding.

Table 2.2. U.S. national-income aggregates, 1997 (billions of dollars per year)

Expenditure categories		Percentage of total output
Personal consumption expenditures	$5,489	_____
Gross private domestic investment	1,238	_____
Exports	959	_____
Imports	1,056	_____
Federal government purchases	525	_____
State and local government purchases	929	_____

2. Are net exports positive or negative in Table 2.2? _____

3. T   F   When net exports are negative, an economy uses more goods and services than it produces.

Exercise 3

The following problem shows how to determine whether a tax is progressive or regressive. It is similar to Problem 5 at the end of Chapter 2 in the text.

Suppose that Table 2.3 describes the spending and saving behavior of individuals at various income levels.

1. Assume that a tax of 40 percent is levied on savings and calculate the following:
    (a) The amount of taxes paid at each income level (column 3 of Table 2.3).
    (b) The fraction of income paid in taxes at each income level (column 4 of Table 2.3).

Table 2.3. Taxes on income and savings

(1) Income	(2) Total savings	(3) Savings tax (at 40 percent)	(4) Savings tax as percentage of income	(5) Income tax (at 10 percent)
$ 1,000	$ −50	$_____	_____%	$_____
2,000	0	_____	_____	_____
3,000	50	_____	_____	_____
5,000	100	_____	_____	_____
10,000	1,000	_____	_____	_____
100,000	20,000	_____	_____	_____

2. Is the tax on savings progressive or regressive in relation to income?
3. Alternatively, assume that a flat-rate income tax of 10 percent is levied. Compute the amount of taxes paid at each income level (column 5 of Table 2.3).
4. Which of the following—a flat-rate income tax or a tax on savings—would provide:
   (a) The most equitable outcome if society wishes to redistribute income to the poor?
   (b) The most equitable outcome if society assumes that everyone should make the same percentage contribution to the maintenance of our government?

Common Errors

The first statement in each "common error" below is incorrect. Each incorrect statement is followed by a corrected version and an explanation.

1. Income and output are two entirely different things. WRONG!
   Income and output are two sides of the same coin. RIGHT!
   This is fundamental. Every time a dollar's worth of final spending takes place, the seller must receive a dollar's worth of income. It could not be otherwise. Remember, profits are used as a balancing item. Don't confuse the term "income" with the term "profit." Profits can be negative, whereas output for the economy cannot.

2. Comparisons of per capita GDP between countries tells you which population is better off. WRONG!
   Comparisons of per capita GDP between countries are only indicators of which population is better off. RIGHT!
   Simple comparisons of per capita GDP ignore how the GDP is distributed. A country with a very high per capita GDP that is unequally distributed may provide a standard of living that is below that of another country with a lower per capita GDP but which is more equally distributed. Other problems with comparisons of per capita GDP result from exchange-rate distortions, differences in mix of output in two countries, and how the economy is organized. GDP per capita is an indicator only of the amount of goods and services each person could have, not what they do have.

3. Equity and equality of income distribution mean the same thing. WRONG!
   Equity and equality of income distribution mean different things. RIGHT!

   Many arguments over the division of the income pie, whether at the national level, the corporate level, or the university level, are laced with the terms *equity* and *equality* used interchangeably. They are not interchangeable. Equality of income distribution means that each person has an equal share. Equity of income distribution implies something about fairness. In a free society some will surely be more productive than others at doing what society wants done. The brain surgeon's services have greater value than the hairdresser's. The surgeon's income will exceed that of the hairdresser—that is, they will be unequal. But is that inequitable? This is a matter of judgment. It's safe to say, however, that if one were not allowed to keep some of the rewards for being more productive than average, our economy would suffer. An equitable distribution of income in our society will require some inequality. How much? There is no sure answer to that question, only a series of compromises.

■ ANSWERS ■

Using Key Terms

Across
3. gross domestic product
4. factors of production
9. exports
11. human capital
12. productivity
14. progressive tax
15. economic growth
16. income transfers
17. capital intensive
18. regressive tax

Down
1. per capita GDP
2. personal distribution of income
5. real GDP
6. in-kind income
7. monopoly
8. imports
10. externality
13. investment

True or False

1. F GDP measures the value of goods and services produced.
2. T
3. F GDP per capita grows when GDP grows more rapidly than population.
4. T
5. T
6. F Manufacturing output has increased since World War II although manufacturing's share of total output in the U.S. has declined.
7. F The great productivity of the U.S. is the result of using highly educated workers in capital-intensive production processes.
8. T
9. T
10. F The U.S. tax system does not play a major role in the redistribution of income because the progressive federal income tax is generally offset by the regressive nature of other taxes.

Multiple Choice

1. b	5. b	9. d	13. d	17. d
2. a	6. b	10. d	14. a	18. b
3. c	7. c	11. a	15. d	19. a
4. d	8. a	12. c	16. a	20. c

26

Problems and Applications

Exercise 1

1. **Table 2.1 Answer**

Year	Real GDP (in billions of dollars per year)	Nominal GDP (in billions of dollars per year)	Percentage growth in real GDP	Percentage growth in nominal GDP	U.S. population (in millions)	Real GDP per capita
1990	6,163.3	5,743.8	----	----	249.9	24,555
1991	6,079.4	5,916.7	−0.9	3.0	252.6	24,067
1992	6,244.4	6,244.4	2.7	5.5	255.4	24,449
1993	6,389.6	6,558.1	2.3	5.0	258.1	24,756
1994	6,610.7	6,947.0	3.5	5.9	260.6	25,367
1995	6,742.1	7,265.4	2.0	4.6	263.0	25,635
1996	6,928.4	7,636.0	2.8	5.1	265.5	26,096
1997	7,191.4	8,083.4	3.8	5.9	267.9	26,844

2. See Table 2.1 answer, columns 5, 6
3. F
4. $2,965.0 billion

5. $1,072.1 billion
6. See Table 2.1 answer, column 8
7. F

Exercise 2

1. **Table 2.2 Answer**

Expenditure categories		Percentage of total output
Personal consumption expenditures	$5,489	67.9
Gross private domestic investment	1,238	15.3
Exports	959	11.9
Imports	1,056	13.1
Federal government purchases	525	6.5
State and local government purchases	929	11.5

2. Negative
3. T

27

Exercise 3

1. a and b.   See columns 3 and 4.

Table 2.3 Answer

(1) Income	(2) Total savings	(3) Savings tax (at 40 percent)	(4) Savings tax as percentage of income	(5) Income tax (at 10 percent)
$ 1,000	$ −50	$ −20	−2.0%	$ 100
2,000	0	0	0.0	200
3,000	50	20	0.67	300
5,000	100	40	0.8	500
10,000	1,000	400	4.0	1,000
100,000	20,000	8,000	8.0	10,000

2.   Progressive. With greater income a higher percentage of income goes to taxes (from 0 to 8 percent in column 4).

3.   See Table 2.3 answer, column 5.

4.   (a)   A progressive tax such as the tax on saving would provide the most equitable outcome if society wishes to redistribute income to the poor.
     (b)   If equity is defined as an equal contribution in terms of percentage of income to the maintenance of government, then the flat-rate income tax would be most equitable.

CHAPTER 3

Supply and Demand

Quick Review

- Participation in the market by consumers, businesses, and government is motivated by the desire to maximize something: utility for consumers, profits for businesses, and general welfare for government.

- Interactions in the marketplace involve either the factor market where factors of production are bought and sold or the product market where goods and services are bought and sold.

- The demand curve represents buyer behavior. It slopes downward and to the right, showing that buyers are willing and able to purchase greater quantities at lower prices, *ceteris paribus*. The supply curve represents producer behavior. It slopes upward and to the right, indicating that producers are willing and able to produce greater quantities at higher prices, *ceteris paribus*.

- Movements along a demand curve result from a change in price. Shifts in a demand curve result from a change in a nonprice determinant—tastes, income, other goods, expectations.

- Movements along a supply curve result from a change in price. Shifts in a supply curve result from a change in a nonprice determinant—technology, factor costs, other goods, taxes and subsidies, expectations, the number of sellers.

- Market demand and market supply summarize the intentions of all those participating on one side of the market or the other.

- Equilibrium price and quantity are established at the intersection of the supply and demand curves. At any price other than the equilibrium price, disequilibrium will occur.

- Price ceilings are set below the equilibrium price and result in shortages; price floors are set above the equilibrium price and result in surpluses. In either case, the market does not clear.

- The market mechanism relies on the free forces of demand and supply to establish market outcomes (prices and quantities) in both product and factor markets. The market mechanism thus can be used to answer the WHAT, HOW, and FOR WHOM questions. This laissez-faire approach requires that government not intervene in the economy.

Learning Objectives

After studying the chapter and doing the following exercises you should:

1. Know the basic questions that must be answered in every economy.
2. Be able to describe the motivations of participants in the product and resource markets.
3. Understand how a demand schedule represents demand and a supply schedule represents supply.
4. Be able to define, graph, and intrepret supply and demand curves.
5. Know the nonprice determinants of both supply and demand and which direction they shift the curves.
6. Understand why it is important to distinguish shifts in supply and demand curves from movements along the curves.
7. Understand how market-supply and market-demand curves are derived from individual supply and demand curves.
8. Know how equilibrium is established and why markets move toward equilibrium.
9. Know the consequences of disequilibrium pricing.
10. Understand the concept of laissez-faire and how free markets provide answers for the WHAT, HOW, and FOR WHOM questions.

Using Key Terms

Fill in the puzzle on the opposite page with the appropriate term from the list of Terms to Remember on page 82 in the text.

Across

3. The result of rent controls discussed on pages 76-78 in the text.
7. Changes from $2.00 to $3.00 in Figure 3.7 in the text.
9. The willingness and ability to sell various quantities of a good at alternative prices.
11. The willingness and ability to buy a particular good at some price.
15. The assumption by economists that nothing else changes.
18. Where businesses purchase the factors of production.
19. Economic policy advocated by Adam Smith.
20. Refers to the inverse relationship between price and quantity.

Down

1. The result of an income change in Figure 3.3 in the text.
2. Will shift in response to a change in taste.
3. The sum of all producers' sales intentions.
4. The result of government intervention in the agricultural markets according to the text.
5. The name of the table from which Figure 3.2 in the text is drawn.
6. Where goods and services are exchanged.
8. The use of market price and sales to signal desired output.
10. The reason for cruise discounts according to the article "Ocean Cruise Prices Relax" in the text.
12. Creates a market surplus.
13. The response of some local governments, including New York City, to high rent prices according to the text.
14. Explains why the curve in Figure 3.5 in the text is upward sloping.
16. The value of the most desirable forgone alternative.
17. What the final curve on the right in Figure 3.4 in the text is called.

Puzzle 3.1

True or False: *Circle your choice and explain why any false statements are incorrect.*

T   F   1.   We rely on others to produce most goods and services for us because we are better off when we specialize in what we produce best and trade for (i.e. purchase) other goods and services.

T   F   2.   A market exists only at those physical locations where exchange takes place.

T   F   3.   The demand curve shows how much of a good a buyer actually purchases at a given price.

T   F   4.   A market-demand curve can be found by adding, horizontally, the demand curves of all the buyers in a given market.

T   F   5.   Sellers' supply curves must take into account consumer demand.

T   F   6.   An increase in the supply of apples occurs when the price of apples increases, *ceteris paribus*.

T   F   7.   The law of supply reflects the concept that it takes a higher price to induce greater output because costs per unit typically increase as output increases.

T   F   8.   There are no shortages or surpluses when the price in a market is equal to the equilibrium price.

T   F   9.   At the equilibrium price of textbooks, everyone that desires a textbook is able to get one.

T   F   10.   When the actual price of a good is greater than the equilibrium price, a surplus results.

Multiple Choice: *Select the correct answer.*

_____   1.   People benefit by participating in the market because:
     (a)   Resources are no longer limited.
     (b)   There is always someone in the market that is more proficient than you at producing a particular good.
     (c)   Market participation allows specialization and, ultimately, higher levels of consumption.
     (d)   Participants in the market do not have to make choices.

_____   2.   The goals of the principal participants in a market economy are to maximize:
     (a)   Income for consumers, profits for businesses, and taxes for government.
     (b)   The quantity of goods and services for consumers, society's welfare for businesses, and taxes for government.
     (c)   Satisfaction from goods and services for consumers, profits for businesses, and society's welfare for government.
     (d)   Society's general welfare.

_____   3.   Consumers (two answers):
     (a)   Provide dollars to the product market.
     (b)   Receive dollars from the product market.
     (c)   Receive dollars from the factor market.
     (d)   Receive goods and services from the factor market.

_____ 4. In the U.S. economy, foreigners participate in:
   (a) Both the product and factor markets.
   (b) The product market only.
   (c) The factor market only.
   (d) Foreigners do not participate in the U.S. economy.

_A_ 5. According to the law of demand, a demand curve:
   (a) Has a negative slope.
   (b) Has a positive slope.
   (c) Is a horizontal, or flat, line.
   (d) Society's demand for goods and services exceeds the economy's ability to produce.

_C_ 6. The determinant of demand that does *not* shift a demand curve is:
   (a) Income.
   (b) Taste.
   (c) The price of the good itself.
   (d) The prices of other goods.

_B_ 7. Given a downward-sloping market demand curve for typing services, if the price of typing services is increased from $8 per hour to $10 per hour, then, *ceteris paribus*:
   (a) The quantity demanded of typing services will increase.
   (b) The quantity demanded of typing services will decrease.
   (c) The demand for typing services will increase.
   (d) The demand for typing services will decrease.

_A-D_ 8. A leftward shift in demand, *ceteris paribus*, is characterized by (two answers):
   (a) A smaller quantity demanded at every price.
   (b) A greater quantity demanded at every price.
   (c) A higher price at each quantity demanded.
   (d) A lower price at each quantity demanded.

_____ 9. Which of the following would generally cause an increase in the demand for automobiles?
   (a) A decrease in the price of automobiles.
   (b) An increase in consumers' income.
   (c) An increase in gasoline prices.
   (d) Consumer expectations that the price of automobiles will be lower next year.

_____ 10. Which of the following best provides an example of the law of supply?
   (a) Falling labor costs cause an increase in supply.
   (b) Improved technology shifts the supply curve to the right.
   (c) Some producers leave the industry, and the supply curve shifts to the left.
   (d) Demand shifts to the left and the quantity supplied decreases.

_B_ 11. A movement along a supply curve is the same as:
   (a) A shift in the supply curve.
   (b) A change in the quantity supplied.
   (c) A change in the quantity demanded.
   (d) All of the above.

12. Which of the following would *not* cause the market supply of telephones to increase?
   (a) Telecommunications are deregulated, and anyone who wants can produce and sell telephones.
   (b) A new and cheaper technology for producing plastics is developed.
   (c) A reduction in the demand for telephones causes their prices to fall.
   (d) Taxes levied on telephone production are reduced.

13. A rightward shift in the supply curve, *ceteris paribus*, is characterized by:
   (a) A smaller quantity supplied and a greater equilibrium price.
   (b) A greater quantity supplied and a greater equilibrium price.
   (c) A smaller quantity supplied and a lower equilibrium price.
   (d) A greater quantity supplied and a lower equilibrium price.

14. A market is said to be in equilibrium when:
   (a) Demand is fully satisfied at all alternative prices.
   (b) The quantity demanded equals the quantity supplied.
   (c) The buying intentions of all consumers are realized.
   (d) The supply intentions of all sellers are realized.

15. In a market, the equilibrium price is determined by:
   (a) What buyers are willing and able to purchase.
   (b) What sellers are willing and able to offer for sale.
   (c) The government.
   (d) Both demand and supply.

16. When demand increases, *ceteris paribus*, the equilibrium price will also increase because:
   (a) A shortage exists at the old equilibrium price.
   (b) A surplus exists at the old equilibrium price.
   (c) The quantity demanded has increased.
   (d) The quantity supplied has decreased.

17. Refer to Figure 3.6 and the accompanying table in the text. If the price per page is $3.00, how many pages are actually sold?
   (a) 90.
   (b) 22.
   (c) 68.
   (d) 39.

18. A market shortage is:
   (a) The amount by which the quantity demanded exceeds the quantity supplied at a given price.
   (b) Caused by a price ceiling.
   (c) A situation in which market price does not equal equilibrium price, so that people cannot buy all of the goods that they are willing and otherwise able to buy.
   (d) All of the above.

34

19. An effective price floor results in pressure to:
    (a) Reduce prices because of surpluses.
    (b) Raise prices because of surpluses.
    (c) Reduce prices because of shortages.
    (d) Raise prices because of shortages.

20. A laissez-faire economic policy would advocate:
    (a) Markets without government interference.
    (b) Price ceilings to make goods and services more affordable for consumers.
    (c) Government determination of WHAT to produce.
    (d) The production of goods and services that are needed rather than demanded.

Problems and Applications

Exercise 1

This exercise provides practice in graphing demand and supply curves for individual buyers and sellers as well as graphing market-demand and market-supply curves.

1. Suppose you were willing and able to buy 20 gallons of gasoline per week if the price were $1 per gallon, but if the price were $3 per gallon you would be willing and able to buy only the bare minimum of 10 gallons. Complete the demand schedule in Table 3.1.

Table 3.1. Your demand schedule for gasoline

Price (dollars per gallon)	Quantity (gallons per week)
$1	_____
3	_____

2. Use your demand schedule for gasoline in Table 3.1 to diagram the demand curve in Figure 3.1. Assume the demand curve is a straight line.

Figure 3.1. Your demand curve for gasoline

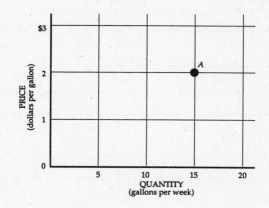

35

If you have drawn the demand curve correctly, it should pass through point *A*.

3. Suppose that 999 other people in your town have demand curves for gasoline that are just like yours in Figure 3.1. Fill out the town's market-demand schedule in Table 3.2 at each price. (Remember to include your own quantity demanded along with everyone else's at each price.)

Table 3.2. Market-demand schedule for gasoline in your town

Price (dollars per gallon)	Quantity (gallons per week)
$1	_____
3	_____

4. Using the market-demand schedule in Table 3.2, draw the market-demand curve for gasoline for your town in Figure 3.2. Assume the curve is a straight line and label it *D*.

Figure 3.2. Market-supply and market-demand curves for gasoline in your town

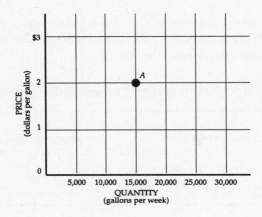

If you have drawn the demand curve correctly, it should pass through point *A*.

5. Suppose the friendly neighborhood gas station is willing to sell 250 gallons at $1 per gallon, and at $3 it is willing to sell 1,250 gallons per week. Fill in the supply schedule for this gas station in Table 3.3.

Table 3.3. Supply schedule for neighborhood gas station

Price (dollars per gallon)	Quantity (gallons per week)
$1	_____
3	_____

6. Graph the supply curve in Figure 3.3 based on the information in Table 3.3 and label it *S*. Assume the supply curve is a straight line.

36

Figure 3.3. Supply curve for neighborhood gas station

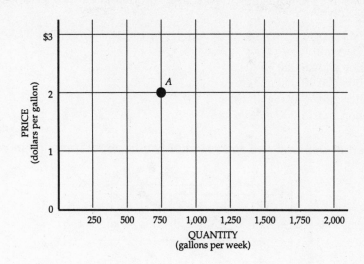

7. Suppose that 19 other gas stations in your town have the same supply schedule as your neighborhood gas station (Table 3.3). Fill out the market-supply schedule for gasoline of the 20 gas stations in your town in Table 3.4.

Table 3.4. Market-demand schedule for gasoline in your town

Price (dollars per gallon)	Quantity (gallons per week)
$1	_____
3	_____

8. Using the market-supply schedule in Table 3.4, draw the market-supply curve for gasoline for your town in Figure 3.2. Assume that the market-supply curve is a straight line. If you have drawn the curve correctly, it should pass through point A. Label the supply curve S.

9. The equilibrium price for gasoline for your town's 20 gas stations and 1,000 buyers of gasoline (see Figure 3.2) is:
   (a) Above $2.
   (b) Exactly $2.
   (c) Below $2.

10. At the equilibrium price:
    (a) There is a shortage.
    (b) There is a surplus.
    (c) There is an excess of inventory.
    (d) The quantity demanded equals the quantity supplied.

Exercise 2

This exercise shows the market mechanics at work in shifting market-demand curves.

1. In Figure 3.4, the supply (S_1) and demand (D_1) curves for gasoline as they might appear in your town are presented. The equilibrium price and quantity are:
    (a) $3 per gallon and 20,000 gallons.
    (b) $2 per gallon and 20,000 gallons.
    (c) $2 per gallon and 15,000 gallons.
    (d) $1 per gallon and 15,000 gallons

Figure 3.4. Market-demand and market-supply curves for gasoline in your town

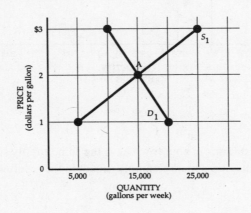

2. Assume that one-half of the people in your town move away. Because of this suppose that the remaining buyers are willing and able to buy only half as much gasoline at each price as was bought before. Draw the new demand curve in Figure 3.4 and label it D_2.

3. When the number of buyers in a market changes, the market-demand curve for goods and services shifts and there is a change in (demand, quantity demanded).

4. When half of the buyers move from your town and the demand curve shifts, the new equilibrium price:
    (a) Is above the old equilibrium price.
    (b) Remains the same as the old equilibrium price.
    (c) Is below the old equilibrium price.
    (*Hint:* See the second demand curve, D_2, in Figure 3.4.)

5. Given the new demand curve, if the market price remains at the old equilibrium price of $2 then:
    (a) A surplus of gasoline will occur.
    (b) A shortage of gasoline will occur.
    (c) The quantity demanded will equal the quantity supplied.

6. When there is a surplus in a market, prices are likely to fall:
    (a) Because buyers do not wish to buy as much as sellers want to sell.
    (b) Because sellers are likely to offer discounts to eliminate expensive excess inventories.
    (c) Because buyers who cannot buy commodities at the current market price are likely to make offers to buy at lower prices that sellers will now accept.
    (d) For all of the above reasons.

7. Whenever there is a leftward shift of the market-demand curve, market forces should push:
   (a) Market prices upward and market quantity downward.
   (b) Market prices upward and market quantity upward.
   (c) Market prices downward and market quantity upward.
   (d) Market prices downward and market quantity downward.

8. Whenever there is a rightward shift of the market-demand curve, market forces should push:
   (a) Market prices upward and market quantity downward.
   (b) Market prices upward and market quantity upward.
   (c) Market prices downward and market quantity upward.
   (d) Market prices downward and market quantity downward.

Exercise 3

This exercise gives practice in computing market-demand and market-supply curves using the demand and supply curves of individuals in a market. It is similar to Problem 3 at the end of the chapter in the text.

1. Table 3.5 shows the weekly demand and supply schedules for various individuals. Fill in the total market quantity that these individuals demand and supply.

Table 3.5. Individual demand and supply schedules

	Price			
	$4	$3	$2	$1
Buyers				
Al's quantity demanded	2	3	5	6
Betsy's quantity demanded	2	2	2	3
Casey's quantity demanded	1	2.5	3	3.5
Total market quantity demanded	_____	_____	_____	_____
Sellers				
Alice's quantity supplied	4	3	2	1
Butch's quantity supplied	6	5	4	2
Connie's quantity supplied	5	4	3	2
Ellen's quantity supplied	5	3	1	0
Total market quantity supplied	_____	_____	_____	_____

Use the data in Table 3.5 to answer Questions 2-4.

2. Construct and label market-supply and market-demand curves in Figure 3.5.

3. Identify the equilibrium point and label it *EQ* in Figure 3.5.

4. What is the situation in terms of quantity demanded versus quantity supplied at a price of $1 in Figure 3.5?

Figure 3.5. Market-supply and market-demand curves for buyers and sellers

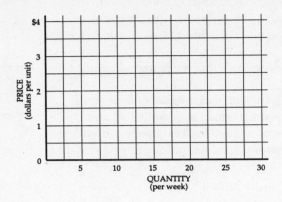

Exercise 4

This exercise provides examples of events that would shift the demand or supply curve. It is similar to Problem 5 at the end of the chapter in the text.

Figure 3.6. Shifts of curves

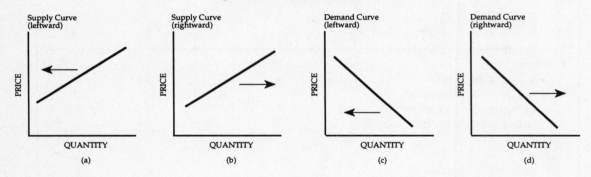

Choose the letter of the appropriate diagram in Figure 3.6 that best describes the shift that would occur in each of the following situations. The shifts are occuring in the market for U.S. defense goods. (*Hint*: Ask yourself if the change first affects buyers or sellers. Refer to the nonprice determinants for demand and supply listed in the text if necessary.)

_____ 1. Because of increased protectionism for steel, steel producers are able to raise the price of speciality steel, which is a key resource in the production of defense goods.

_____ 2. A new superior engineering design is developed that reduces the amount of materials needed to produce nuclear submarines.

_____ 3. New buyers enter the market to purchase defense goods.

_____ 4. A large firm in the defense industry closes down when it loses a defense contract.

_____ 5. A country that previously bought U.S. defense goods enters into a peace agreement.

Common Errors

The first statement in each "common error" below is incorrect. Each incorrect statement is followed by a corrected version and an explanation.

1. Market price is the same thing as equilibrium price. WRONG!
   The market price moves by trial and error (via the market mechanism) toward the equilibrium price. RIGHT!

   When demand and supply curves shift, the market is temporarily out of equilibrium. The price may move along a demand or supply curve toward the new equilibrium.

2. Since the quantity bought must equal the quantity sold, every market is always in equilibrium by definition. WRONG!
   Although quantity bought equals quantity sold, there may be shortages or surpluses. RIGHT!

   Although the quantity *actually* bought does equal the quantity *actually* sold, there may still be buyers who *are willing and able* to buy more of the good at the market price (shortages exist) or sellers who are willing and able to sell more of the good at the market price (surpluses exist). If the market price is above the equilibrium price, there will be a surplus of goods (inventories). Prices will be lowered by sellers toward the equilibrium price. If the market price is below the equilibrium price, there will be a shortage of goods. Prices will be bid up by buyers toward the equilibrium price.

3. A change in price changes the demand for goods by consumers. WRONG!
   A change in price changes the quantity demanded by consumers in a given time period. RIGHT!

   Economists differentiate between the terms "quantity demanded" and "demand." A change in the quantity demanded refers to a movement along the demand curve due to a change in the price of the good itself. A change in demand refers to a shift of the demand curve due to a change in tastes, income, price and availability of other goods, or expectations.

4. A change in price changes the supply of goods produced by a firm. WRONG!
   A change in price changes the quantity of a good supplied by a firm in a given time period. RIGHT!

   Economists differentiate between the terms "quantity supplied" and "supply." A change in the quantity supplied refers to a movement along a supply curve due to a change in price. A change in supply refers to a shift of the supply curve due to a change in technology, factor costs, other goods, taxes and subsidies, expectations, or number of sellers.

■ ANSWERS ■

Using Key Terms

Across
3. market shortage
7. equilibrium price
9. supply
11. demand
15. *ceteris paribus*
18. factor market
19. laissez faire
20. law of demand

Down
1. shift in demand
2. demand curve
3. market supply
4. government failure
5. demand schedule
6. product market
8. market mechanism
10. market surplus
12. price floor
13. price ceiling
14. law of supply
16. opportunity cost
17. market demand

True or False

1. T
2. F   A market exists whenever exchange takes place. Exchange can take place over the phone, by mail, or on the Internet, not just in physical locations.
3. F   A demand curve only shows how much consumers are willing and able to purchase. The amount they actually buy also depends on supply.
4. T
5. F   Supply represents the intentions of the sellers only, i.e. the quantities of goods they are willing and able to offer for sale at various prices.
6. F   An increase in quantity supplied occurs when the price of apples increases. This results in a movement along the supply curve.
7. T
8. T
9. F   Only those buyers that can afford the equilibrium price will be able to get a textbook.
10. T

Multiple Choice

1. c	5. a	9. b	13. d	17. b
2. c	6. c	10. d	14. b	18. d
3. a, c	7. b	11. b	15. d	19. a
4. a	8. a, d	12. c	16. a	20. a

Problems and Applications

Exercise 1

1. **Table 3.1 Answer**

p	q
$1	20
3	10

2. **Figure 3.1 Answer**

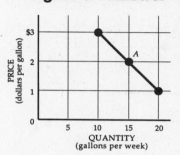

3. **Table 3.2 Answer**

p	q
$1	20,000
3	10,000

4. **Figure 3.2 Answer**

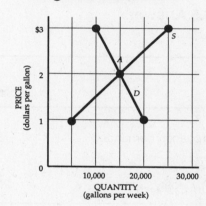

5. **Table 3.3 Answer**

p	q
$1	250
3	1,250

6. **Figure 3.3 Answer**

7. **Table 3.4 Answer**

p	q
$1	5,000
3	25,000

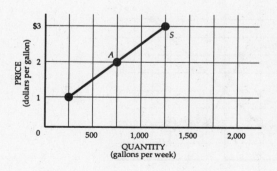

8. See Figure 3.2 answer
9. b
10. d

43

Exercise 2

1. c

2. **Figure 3.4 Answer**

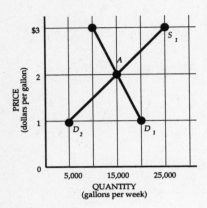

3. Demand
4. c
5. a
6. d
7. d
8. b

Exercise 3

1. **Table 3.5 Answer**

	Price			
	$4	$3	$2	$1
Buyers Total market quantity demanded	5	7.5	10	12.5
Sellers Total market quantity supplied	20	15	10	5

2. **Figure 3.5 Answer**

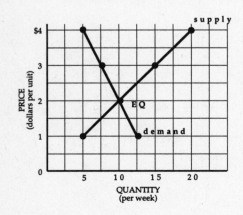

3. See point *EQ* in Figure 3.5.
4. The quantity demanded is greater than the quantity supplied or there is a shortage of 7.5 units (12.5 minus 5).

Exercise 4

1. a
2. b
3. d
4. a
5. c

CHAPTER 4

Consumer Demand

Quick Review

- Economic theory focuses on demand—our willingness and ability to buy specific quantities of a good at various prices—and does not try to explain why people want the things they do.

- Utility is the satisfaction obtained from a particular good. Total utility is the total amount of satisfaction we get from consuming a given quantity of a good; marginal utility is the satisfaction we get from consuming the last unit.

- The law of diminishing marginal utility says that the more we consume of a product or service, the smaller the increments of satisfaction we get from consuming additional units. This provides the basis for the law of demand. Marginal utility must be related to price to derive the law of demand.

- The law of demand says that we will buy more of a good at lower prices than we will at higher prices, *ceteris paribus*. The nonprice determinants of demand—tastes, income, expectations, and the price and availability of other goods—are held constant when we draw a demand curve. If any of these change, the demand curve shifts.

- Price elasticity of demand is a measure of the responsiveness of quantity demanded to a given change in price. It is calculated between two points on a given demand curve by dividing the percentage change in quantity demanded by the percentage change in price that brought it about.

- The coefficient (E) that results from the elasticity calculation is always negative because of the law of demand, so we use its absolute value to interpret its meaning. If $|E| > 1$, we call it elastic; $|E| < 1$, inelastic; $|E| = 1$, unitary elastic.

- Price elasticity determines the impact of a price change on total revenue ($P \times Q$). If price falls and demand is elastic, total revenue will increase; if price falls and demand is inelastic, total revenue will decrease. The reverse is true for price increases.

- The determinants of price elasticity are the price of the good relative to income, the availability of substitutes, and the time available to adjust purchases.

- Advertising is intended to influence the willingness of the consumer to purchase a good and thus shift the demand curve.

Learning Objectives

After studying the chapter and doing the following exercises, you should:

1. Be able to distinguish the demand for a good from the desire for it.
2. Understand the concept of utility and the relationship between total utility and marginal utility.
3. Understand the relationship between the law of diminishing marginal utility and the law of demand.
4. Be able to compute and interpret the price elasticity of demand coefficient.
5. Understand the relationship between elasticity and total revenue when price changes.
6. Know the determinants of price elasticity and how they influence the elasticity coefficient.
7. Understand how advertising causes the demand curve to shift.

Using Key Terms

Fill in the puzzle on the opposite page with the appropriate term from the list of Terms to Remember on page 101 in the text.

Across

3. In the cartoon on page 92 in the text, the fourth hamburger does not provide as much satisfaction as the first hamburger because of the law of _____.
5. Explains why the curve in Figure 4.4 in the text is downward sloping.
9. According to the article "What is Water Worth?" in the text, this value is" enormous" for water.
10. Influenced by tastes, income, expectations, and other goods.
11. The quantity of a product sold times the price at which it is sold.

Down

1. Measures the response of consumers to a change in price.
2. Positive but diminishing for the first five boxes of popcorn in Figure 4.3 in the text.
4. The assumption that everything else is constant.
6. The sum of individual demands.
7. Satisfaction obtained from goods and services.
8. Affected by advertising in Figure 4.6 in the text.

Puzzle 4.1

True or False: *Circle your choice and explain why any false statements are incorrect.*

T   F   1. It is the economist's job to explain why consumers desire certain goods and services.

T   F   2. An expected price change has the same effect on demand as a change in the current price.

T   F   3. When the price of apples decreases, the demand for pears (a substitute) also decreases.

T   F   4. The law of demand differs from the law of diminishing marginal utility in that it takes into account what a consumer is able to pay for a good, not just the consumer's desire for the good.

T   F   5. As a consumer eats more candy bars, for example, the consumer's total satisfaction decreases, according to the law of diminishing marginal utility.

T   F   6. The price elasticity of demand is said to be elastic when the percentage change in the quantity demanded of a good is greater than the percentage change in the good's price.

T   F   7. If the price elasticity of demand is equal to 1.5, then a 1 percent increase in price will result in a 1.5 percent decrease in quantity demanded.

T   F   8. If the price elasticity of demand is inelastic, an increase in the price increases both total revenue and quantity demanded.

T   F   9. The price elasticity of demand for Pepsi is more elastic than the price elasticity of demand for sodas in general.

T   F   10. A successful advertising campaign increases the marginal utility consumers receive from a product.

Multiple Choice: *Select the correct answer.*

_____ 1. The difference between demanding a good and desiring a good is:
   (a) Goods that are demanded are goods that are needed to survive while goods that are desired are typically luxuries.
   (b) Consumers not only desire, but also are able to pay for demanded goods.
   (c) Desired goods typically sell at a higher price than demanded goods.
   (d) Goods that are demanded have a more price inelastic demand than goods that are desired.

_____ 2. Which of the following are possible explanations for how much a consumer demands a particular good?
   (a) The consumers ability to pay.
   (b) The consumer's fears, psychological complexes, and anxieties.
   (c) Ego and status.
   (d) All of the above.

3. According to Figure 4.1 in the text, the typical consumer spends most of his or her income on:
   (a) Food.
   (b) Medical care.
   (c) Transportation.
   (d) Housing.

4. *Ceteris paribus* means (in demand theory):
   (a) Nothing is allowed to change.
   (b) The determinants of demand may change, but all else must be held constant.
   (c) Only one determinant is being changed while all other determinants remain unchanged.
   (d) Consumers try to keep all things constant so that prices will be lower.

5. Suppose that a man loses his job and is unable to find another. Which of the following is most likely to occur?
   (a) His demand curve for goods and services will shift to the left.
   (b) His demand curve for goods and services will shift to the right.
   (c) He will move up along his demand curve for goods and services.
   (d) He will move down along his demand curve for goods and services.

6. The market demand curve is calculated by:
   (a) Summing the quantities demanded from individual demand curves.
   (b) Averaging the quantities demanded from individual demand curves.
   (c) Summing the prices from individual demand curves.
   (d) Averaging the prices from individual demand curves.

7. Which of the following statements best illustrates the law of diminishing marginal utility?
   (a) Broccoli gives me no satisfaction, so I won't spend my income for any of it.
   (b) The more soda I drink, the more I want to drink.
   (c) The more I go to school, the more I want to do something else.
   (d) Since we need water more than we need diamonds, water is more valuable.

8. The amount of satisfaction obtained from the consumption of an additional unit of a good or service is:
   (a) Never negative.
   (b) Total utility.
   (c) A function of supply.
   (d) Marginal utility.

9. With greater consumption, total utility:
   (a) Falls.
   (b) Increases.
   (c) Increases as long as marginal utility is positive.
   (d) Increases only if marginal utility increases.

10. If the marginal utility that Maggie receives from additional pretzels is decreasing then:
    (a) Maggie's total utility for pretzels may be decreasing.
    (b) Maggie's total utility for pretzels may be increasing.
    (c) Maggie's marginal utility may be negative.
    (d) All of the above could be correct.

11. A change in a determinant of demand for a good causes:
    (a) A shift in demand.
    (b) A change in marginal utility.
    (c) A change in a consumer's willingness or ability to buy the good.
    (d) All of the above could be correct.

12. Refer to the Headline article on page 92 in the text. Which of the following is the best reason why we typically pay a relatively low price for water?
    (a) Additional units of water are normally not worth much to us.
    (b) Because water is normally abundant, the total utility we receive from water is relatively low.
    (c) Because water is normally abundant, the marginal utility we receive from water is relatively high.
    (d) Although additional units of water are normally worth a lot to us, the supply of water is so great we refuse to pay a high price for these additional units.

13. If a good has a zero price (i.e., is free), a consumer should consume:
    (a) An infinite amount of the good.
    (b) The good until total utility is zero.
    (c) The good until the marginal utility of the last unit is zero.
    (d) The good until marginal utility of the last unit is maximized.

14. The concept of elasticity:
    (a) Compares the absolute change in quantity demanded with the percentage change in price.
    (b) Provides evidence of the way total revenue changes when price changes.
    (c) Shows what the slope of the demand curve is.
    (d) Does both a and c.

15. Suppose that a local government desires to reduce traffic congestion on a highway bridge by imposing a toll. The toll will be most effective if the price elasticity of demand for the bridge is:
    (a) Inelastic.
    (b) Elastic.
    (c) Unitary.
    (d) Impossible to tell without more information on, for example, substitute routes available.

16. When a firm raises the price of its product, total revenue will:
    (a) Always increase because the firm is receiving more revenue per unit sold.
    (b) Always decrease because the firm is selling fewer units.
    (c) Only rise if the increase in revenue from the higher price more than makes up for the decrease in revenue from the lower quantity sold.
    (d) Increase if the price elasticity of demand is elastic.

17. One of the airline industry's arguments against deregulation of airfares was that the resulting fall in prices would lower total revenue for the industry. Instead, total revenue rose. Assuming the increase in total revenue was due solely to the lower fares, it can be concluded that:
    (a) Airline representatives thought demand for plane trips was elastic.
    (b) Quantity demanded of airline service increased by a greater percentage than the percentage fall in price.
    (c) Demand for airline service increased with the fall in prices.
    (d) Airlines were more profitable after deregulation.

18. Refer to the Headline article in the text on page 96. If the tobacco lobby was successful in lowering the price of cigarettes by 25 percent, by what percentage would the quantity sold change? Assume a price elasticity of demand of 0.65.
    (a) Decrease by 6.50 percent.
    (b) Decrease by 25.00 percent.
    (c) Increase by 16.25 percent.
    (d) Increase by 2.60 percent.

19. Refer to the table in Figure 4.5 in the text. Between the prices of $0.50 and $0.25, the price elasticity of demand for this good is:
    (a) Elastic.
    (b) Inelastic.
    (c) Unitary elastic.
    (d) Can not be determined with the information given.

20. When a firm advertises, it is attempting to:
    (a) Increase the demand for its product.
    (b) Increase the marginal utility consumers receive from the product.
    (c) Decrease the price elasticity of demand for the product.
    (d) All of the above are correct.

Problems and Applications

Exercise 1

This exercise will help you to draw demand curves from demand schedules. It should also give you practice in constructing market-demand curves.

1. Market demand is:
    (a) The total quantity of a good or service that people are willing and able to buy at alternative prices in a given period of time, *ceteris paribus*.
    (b) The sum of individual demands.
    (c) Represented as the horizontal sum of individual demand curves.
    (d) All of the above.

2. Table 4.1 presents a *hypothetical* demand schedule for cars manufactured in the United States.

Table 4.1. Demand for U.S. cars

Price	Number of new U.S. cars (millions per year)
$10,000	9.0
9,000	10.0

Graph this demand curve in Figure 4.1.

Figure 4.1

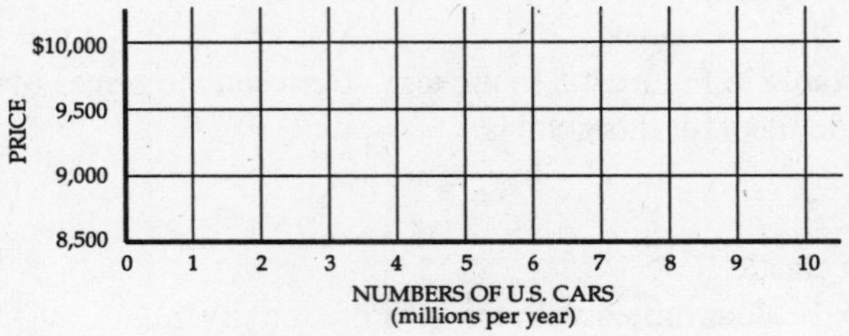

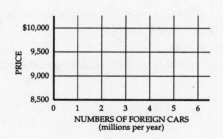

3. Table 4.2 presents a similar demand schedule for imported cars.

Table 4.2. Demand for foreign cars

Price	Number of new foreign cars (millions per year)
$10,000	1.0
9,000	2.0

Graph this demand curve in Figure 4.2.

Figure 4.2

54

4. Suppose that foreign-car prices are always kept competitive with domestic-car prices, so that they are the same. In Table 4.3 calculate the demand schedule for cars (both foreign and domestically produced) at the two prices shown.

Table 4.3. Market demand for new cars

Price	Number of new cars (millions per year)
$10,000	_____
9,000	_____

5. In Figure 4.3 draw the domestic market-demand curve for both foreign and domestic cars.

Figure 4.3

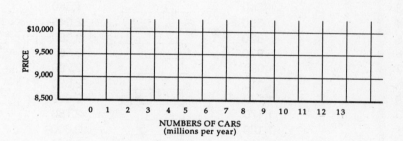

Exercise 2

This exercise shows the relationship between total and marginal utility. It also gives practice in identifying the law of diminishing marginal utility.

Suppose there are two types of entertainment you enjoy—an evening at home with friends and an "event" entertainment, such as a sports event or a rock concert. The number of times that you experience each type of entertainment during a month determines the total utility of each type of entertainment for that month. Suppose Table 4.4 represents the total utility you achieve from consuming various quantities of the two types of entertainment.

1. Compute the marginal utility of each type of entertainment by completing Table 4.4.

Table 4.4. Total and marginal utility of two types of entertainment per month

Days of entertainment per month	Evening at home		Event	
	Total utility	Marginal utility	Total utility	Marginal utility
0	0	_____	0	_____
1	170	_____	600	_____
2	360	_____	1,250	_____
3	540	_____	1,680	_____
4	690	_____	2,040	_____
5	820	_____	2,350	_____
6	930	_____	2,550	_____
7	1,030	_____	2,720	_____
8	1,110	_____	2,820	_____
9	1,170	_____	2,820	_____
10	1,170	_____	2,760	_____
11	1,120	_____	2,660	_____
12	1,020	_____	2,460	_____

2. The law of diminishing marginal utility means:
   (a) The total utility of a good declines as more of it is consumed in a given time period.
   (b) The marginal utility of a good declines as more of it is consumed in a given time period.
   (c) The price of a good declines as more of it is consumed in a given period of time.
   (d) All of the above.

3. The law of diminishing marginal utility is in evidence in Table 4.4:
   (a) For both types of entertainment.
   (b) For home entertainment only.
   (c) For event entertainment only.
   (d) For neither type of entertainment.
   (*Hint*: You should be able to tell by looking at the marginal utility columns in Table 4.4. Does the marginal utility become smaller as you go down the column?)

4. In Figure 4.4 graph the total utility curve for evenings at home.

Figure 4.4

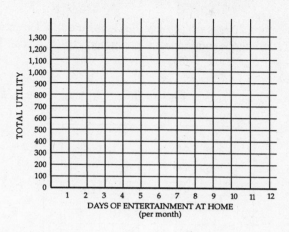

5. In Figure 4.5 graph the marginal utility curve for evenings at home.

Figure 4.5

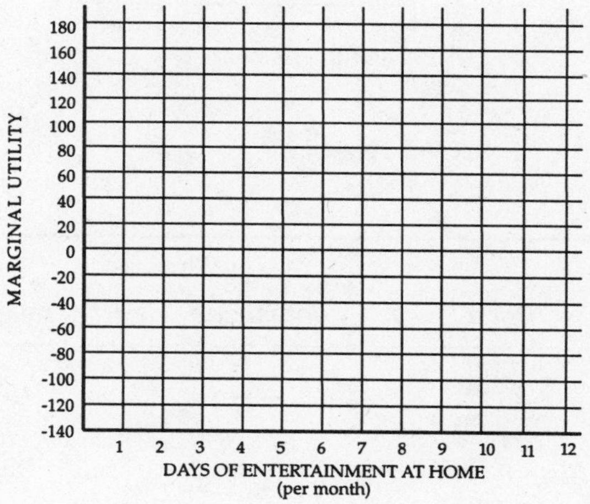

6. On the basis of the two graphs, marginal utility becomes zero only when:
    (a) Total utility is zero.
    (b) Total utility reaches a maximum.
    (c) Total utility is rising.
    (d) Total utility is falling.

7. When total utility is rising, then:
    (a) Marginal utility is rising.
    (b) Marginal utility is negative.
    (c) Marginal utility is positive.
    (d) Marginal utility is zero.

Exercise 3

This exercise examines the relationship between the price elasticity of demand and total revenue.

1. Figure 4.6 shows the demand curve for a good. Find the quantity demanded of the good for each price given in Table 4.5. Calculate the total revenue generated at each price. Then use Table 4.5 to answer Questions 2-5.

Figure 4.6

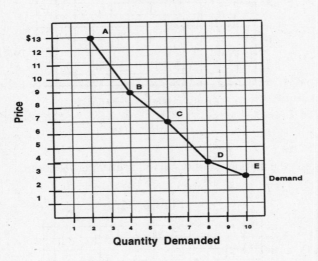

Quantity Demanded

Table 4.5

	Price	X	Quantity demanded	=	Total revenue
A	$ 13.00		_____		_____
B	9.00		_____		_____
C	7.00		_____		_____
D	4.00		_____		_____
E	3.00		_____		_____

2. T   F   The price elasticity of demand is used to measure the response of consumers to a change in price.

3. As price decreases from $4.00 per unit to $3.00 per unit total revenue (increases, decreases, stays the same). In this case the price elasticity of demand is (elastic, inelastic, unitary elastic).

4. As price decreases from $13.00 per unit to $9.00 per unit total revenue (increases, decreases, stays the same). In this case the price elasticity of demand is (elastic, inelastic, unitary elastic).

58

5. The price elasticity of demand is influenced by:
   (a) The price of the good relative to income.
   (b) The availability of substitutes.
   (c) Time.
   (d) All of the above.

Common Errors

The first statement in each "common error" below is incorrect. Each incorrect statement is followed by a corrected version and an explanation.

1. The law of demand and the law of diminishing marginal utility are the same. WRONG!
   The law of demand and the law of diminishing marginal utility are not the same. RIGHT!
   Do not confuse utility and demand. Utility refers only to expected satisfaction.
   Demand refers to both preferences and ability to pay. This distinction should help you to keep the law of diminishing marginal utility separate from the law of demand.
2. Figures 4.7a and 4.7b represent simple graphs drawn from a demand schedule.

Figure 4.7a

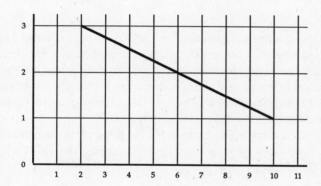

Price (dollars per unit)	Output quantity per unit of time
10	1
2	3

WRONG!

Figure 4.7b

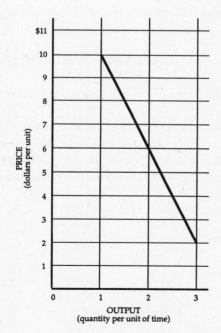

Price (dollars per unit)	Output quantity per unit of time
10	1
2	3

RIGHT!

59

The first graph has been drawn without any units indicated. It is something of an accidental tradition in economics to show price on the y-axis and quantity on the x-axis. This convention is sometimes confusing to mathematicians, who want to treat quantity as a function of price, according to the definition in the text. In Figure 4.7a the axes have been reversed and incorrect points have been chosen.

Be careful! When you are drawing a new graph, pay special attention to the label for each axis and the units of measure used on each axis. If you are drawing a graph from a table (or schedule), you can usually determine what should be on the axes by looking at the heading above the column from which you are reading the numbers.

Make sure price is shown on the y-axis (vertical) and quantity on the x-axis (horizontal). If you mix up the two, you may confuse a graph showing elastic demand with one showing inelastic demand.

3. The formula for the price elasticity of demand is:

$$\frac{\text{Change in price}}{\text{Change in quantity}} \qquad \qquad \text{WRONG!}$$

The formula for the price elasticity of demand is:

$$\frac{\text{Percentage change in quantity}}{\text{Percentage change in price}} \qquad \qquad \text{RIGHT!}$$

The concept of elasticity allows us to compare relative changes in quantity and price without having to worry about the units in which they are measured. In order to do this, we compute percentage changes of both price and quantity. A change in price *causes* people to change the quantity they demand in a given time period. By putting the quantity changes in the numerator, we can see that if the quantity response is very large in relation to a price change, the elasticity will also be very large. If the quantity response is small in relation to a price change, then demand is inelastic (elasticity is small).

Be careful! Do not confuse slope and elasticity. The formula for the slope of the demand curve is the *wrong* formula shown above. The formula for the price elasticity of demand is the *right* formula. Remember to take the absolute value of the elasticity too.

4. A flat demand curve has an elasticity of zero. WRONG!
    A flat demand curve has an infinite elasticity. RIGHT!

When price remains constant even when quantity changes, the elasticity formula requires us to divide by a zero price change. In fact, as demand curves approach flatness, the elasticity becomes larger and larger. By agreement we say it is infinite.

5. The expectation that price will change in the future has the same effect as a change in the current price. WRONG!
    The expectation that price will change in the future shifts the demand curve, whereas a current price change is a movement along the demand curve. RIGHT!

If prices are expected to rise in the near future, people will demand more of the commodity today in order to beat the rise in price. Demand increases and the quantity demanded will rise. However, if the price rises today, according to the law of demand, people will reduce their quantity demanded! Furthermore, demand itself does not change. A current price change and an expected price change have very different effects.

■ ANSWERS ■

Using Key Terms

Across
3. diminishing marginal utility
5. law of demand
9. total utility
10. demand
11. total revenue

Down
1. price elasticity of demand
2. marginal utility
4. *ceteris paribus*
6. market demand
7. utility
8. demand curve

True or False

1. F It is the economist's job to explain why consumers demand certain goods and services.
2. F An expected price change will shift the demand curve while a change in the current price will result in a movement along a demand curve.
3. T
4. T
5. F According to the law of diminishing marginal utility, marginal satisfaction (i.e. utility) decreases as consumption increases. Total utility increases until marginal utility becomes negative.
6. T
7. T
8. F An increase in the price would cause total revenue to increase but quantity demanded to decrease.
9. T
10. T

Multiple Choice

1. b	5. a	9. c	13. c	17. b
2. d	6. a	10. d	14. b	18. c
3. d	7. c	11. d	15. b	19. a
4. c	8. d	12. a	16. c	20. d

Problems and Applications

Exercise 1

1. d

2. **Figure 4.1 Answer**

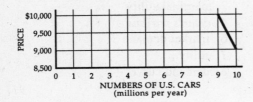

3. **Figure 4.2 Answer**

4. **Table 4.3 Answer**

Price	Number of new cars (millions per year)
$10,000	10.00
9,000	12.00

5. **Figure 4.3 Answer**

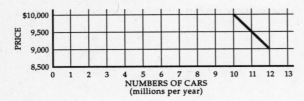

Exercise 2

1. **Table 4.4 Answer**

Days of entertainment per month	Evening at home Marginal utility	Event Marginal utility
0	—	—
1	170	600
2	190	650
3	180	430
4	150	360
5	130	310
6	110	200
7	100	170
8	80	100
9	60	0
10	0	−60
11	−50	−100
12	−100	−200

2. b

3. a

4. **Figure 4.4 Answer**

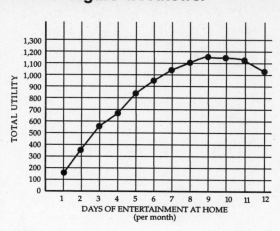

5. **Figure 4.5 Answer**

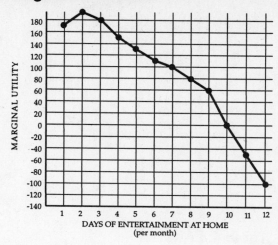

6. b
7. c

Exercise 3

1. **Table 4.5 Answer**

	Quantity demanded	Total revenue
A	2	$26.00
B	4	36.00
C	6	42.00
D	8	32.00
E	10	30.00

2. T
3. Decreases; inelastic
4. Increases; elastic
5. d

CHAPTER 5

Supply Decisions

Quick Review

- The supply decision begins with the production function that determines how much output can be obtained from varying amounts of factor inputs. Every point on the production function is efficient, meaning that, given current technology, the maximum output is being produced.

- The output of any factor depends on the amount of other resources available to it. Fixed factors constrain the firm's ability to produce output. As more of a variable input is applied to a fixed input, at some point, the marginal physical product of the variable input begins to get smaller in size. This short-run situation is referred to as the law of diminishing returns. In the long run, all factor inputs are variable.

- The dollar costs incurred because of fixed inputs are called fixed costs; those for variable factors are called variable costs. In the short-run, even if output is zero, there are fixed costs. The total cost of producing any level of output is the sum of fixed and variable costs. Because fixed costs do not change as output changes, the rate of increase in total cost is determined by variable costs only.

- Average total cost (ATC) is the total cost of production divided by the rate of output. Marginal cost (MC) is the increase in total cost associated with a one-unit increase in production. The ATC curve starts at a high level and declines as production increases because of fixed costs. At a point the ATC curve begins to rise because of rising marginal costs which result from the law of diminishing returns. The MC curve always intersects the ATC curve at its minimum.

- Economic costs include both explicit and implicit costs associated with the use of *all* resources exhausted in the production process, whether they receive a monetary payment or not. Accounting costs include only those for which an explicit payment is made.

- The production decision is the short-run choice of how much output to produce with existing facilities. A producer will be willing to supply output only if price at least covers marginal costs.

- In the long run there are no fixed costs. The producer must decide whether to build, buy, or lease plant and equipment. This is the investment decision.

- Advances in technology shift the production function upward and the cost curves downward. Along with improved quality of inputs, technology improvements have historically been the major source of productivity growth in the U.S. economy.

Learning Objectives

After studying the chapter and doing the following exercises you should:

1. Know the relationship between the production function and the firm's ability to produce an output.
2. Be able to define and explain the law of diminishing returns.
3. Understand the importance of the distinction between the short run and the long run.
4. Understand the relationship between the production function and the short-run cost curves.
5. Be able to distinguish fixed costs from variable costs in the production process.
6. Be able to calculate the total, average, and marginal costs of production and understand how they relate to each other.
7. Understand the difference between implicit costs and explicit costs; economic costs and ac counting costs.
8. Be able to distinguish the production decision from the investment decision.
9. Understand how technological improvements affect the production function and cost curves.

Using Key Terms

Fill in the puzzle on the opposite page with the appropriate term from the list of Terms to Remember on page 123 in the text.

Across

2. This economic principle was experienced in the factories of communist nations according to the article, "We Pretend to Work, They Pretend to Pay Us."
3. Used in Table 5.1 in the text to tell us how the output of jeans would change if some sewing machines were leased.
4. The resources used to produce a good or service.
8. The horizontal curve at $120 in Figure 5.2 in the text.
11. The difference between total revenue and total costs.
13. Includes both explicit and implicit costs.
14. The ability and willingness to produce a good at various prices.
15. Drawn with a U-shape in Figure 5.3 in the text.

Down

1. Equal to 15 for the first worker hired in Figure 5.1 in the text.
3. The selection of the short-run rate of output.
5. The choice being made by Texas Instruments in the Headline on page 121 in the text.
6. A period in which some inputs are fixed.
7. This curve is typically rising because of the law of diminishing returns.
9. Equals $245 when producing 15 pairs of jeans per day according to Table 5.2 in the text.
10. Determine how fast total costs rise.
12. A period in which all inputs are variable.

Puzzle 5.1

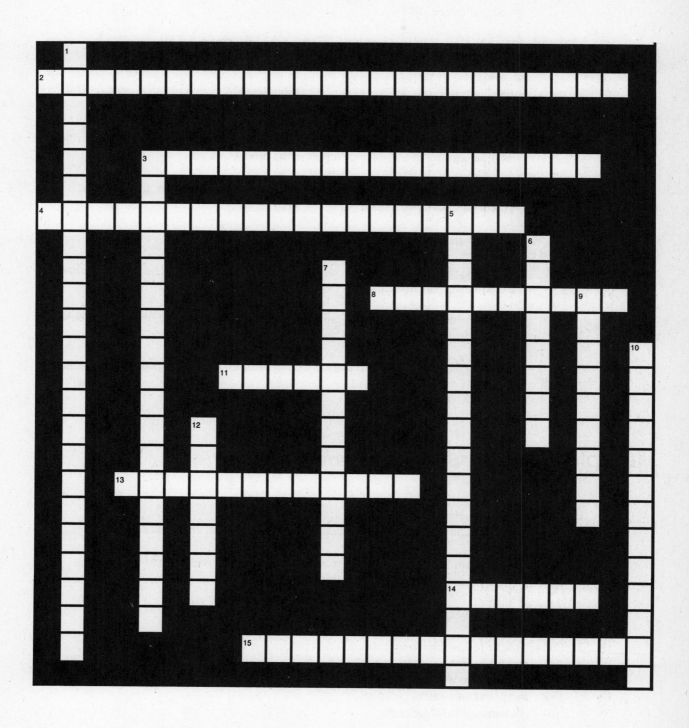

True or False: *Circle your choice and explain why any false statements are incorrect.*

T F 1. According to the text, the average U.S. producer earns a profit of about 10 to 12 percent.

T F 2. A production function tells us the maximum amount of output that can be produced with one factor input.

T F 3. The production function of a company would shift upward if the company's workers produced to their maximum efficiency.

T F 4. Total output may continue to rise even though the marginal physical product (MPP) is decreasing.

T F 5. The marginal physical product (MPP) will eventually begin to decline because of the relative scarcity of some factor inputs in the production process.

T F 6. If any factor inputs are fixed in a firm's decision-making process, then the firm is making a short-run decision.

T F 7. In the short run, when output is zero total costs are zero.

T F 8. When the marginal physical product (MPP) curve shifts upward because of technological advances, the marginal cost (MC) curve shifts downward.

T F 9. When the cost of an additional unit of output (MC) is increasing, the average cost per unit of output (ATC) must also be increasing.

T F 10. Economic costs exist only if an explicit payment for a factor of production is made.

Multiple Choice: *Select the correct answer.*

_____ 1. A production function shows:
(a) The minimum amount of output that can be obtained from alternative combinations of inputs.
(b) The maximum quantity of inputs required to produce a given quantity of output.
(c) The maximum quantity of output that can be obtained from alternative combinations of inputs.
(d) The maximum profit that a firm can earn.

_____ 2. Which of the following would cause a firm's production function to shift upward?
(a) An increase in production by the firm.
(b) Hiring more workers.
(c) Increased investment in capital.
(d) An increase in factor costs.

_____ 3. Assuming labor is a variable input, an increase in labor productivity would result in:
   (a) An upward shift in the MPP curve.
   (b) A downward shift in the MC curve.
   (c) A downward shift in the ATC curve.
   (d) All of the above are correct.

_____ 4. The law of diminishing returns begins to occur when:
   (a) Total output begins to decline.
   (b) Marginal physical product becomes negative.
   (c) Total output begins to rise.
   (d) Marginal physical product begins to decline.

_____ 5. Declining MPP is the result of:
   (a) Inefficiency in the production process.
   (b) Adding more variable factors of production to a fixed quantity of other factors of production.
   (c) Laziness on the part of the workers.
   (d) The use of less qualified workers.

_____ 6. Refer to Table 5.1 in the text and fill in the blank in the following sentence. When the company is leasing 2 sewing machines, the law of diminishing returns takes effect when the _____ worker is added to the production process.
   (a) First
   (b) Third
   (c) Fifth
   (d) Eighth

_____ 7. Which of the following is the best explanation of why the law of diminishing returns does not apply in the long run?
   (a) In the long run, firms can increase the availability of space and equipment to keep up with the increase in labor.
   (b) The MPP does not change in the long run.
   (c) In the long run, firms have more time to find better-qualified workers.
   (d) All factors of production are fixed in the long run.

_____ 8. The most desirable rate of output for a firm is the output that:
   (a) Minimizes total costs.
   (b) Maximizes total profit.
   (c) Minimizes marginal costs.
   (d) Maximizes total revenue.

_____ 9. Which of the following costs will always increase as output increases?
   (a) Total costs.
   (b) Average total costs.
   (c) Marginal costs.
   (d) Fixed costs.

10. Which of the following is equivalent to total cost?
    (a) Change in total cost divided by change in output.
    (b) 1 / MPP.
    (c) Fixed costs + variable costs.
    (d) Marginal costs + variable costs.

11. Changes in short-run total costs result from changes in:
    (a) Variable costs.
    (b) Fixed costs.
    (c) Profit.
    (d) The price elasticity of demand.

12. Marginal cost:
    (a) Is the change in total cost from producing one additional unit of output.
    (b) Is the change in total variable cost from producing one additional unit of output.
    (c) Rises because of declining marginal physical product.
    (d) All of the above.

13. Which of the following would most likely be a fixed cost?
    (a) The cost of property insurance.
    (b) The cost of water used in the production process.
    (c) The cost of labor used in the production process.
    (d) The cost of electricity used in the production process.

14. Rising marginal costs are the result of:
    (a) The law of diminishing returns.
    (b) Decreasing MPP.
    (c) Adding more variable factors of production to a fixed quantity of other factors of production.
    (d) All of the above are correct.

15. Refer to the table in Figure 5.3 in the text. The marginal cost of the 51st unit of output is:
    (a) $753.
    (b) $1.36.
    (c) $83.
    (d) $0, because fixed costs do not change.

16. Which of the following costs must remain constant at all levels of output?
    (a) Total costs.
    (b) Variable costs.
    (c) Fixed costs.
    (d) Marginal costs.

17. Which of the following can you compute if you know total cost at all levels of output?
    (a) Fixed cost.
    (b) Variable cost.
    (c) Marginal cost.
    (d) All of the above.

18. Which of the following curves must be rising when the marginal cost curve is above it?
    (a)   Fixed cost.
    (b)   Average total cost.
    (c)   Total cost.
    (d)   Marginal physical product.

19. Economic and accounting costs will differ whenever:
    (a)   There is more than one factor of production.
    (b)   A factor used by the firm is not explicitly paid for by the firm.
    (c)   There are no implicit costs incurred by the firm.
    (d)   All factors of production are free to the firm.

20. The planning period over which at least one resource input is fixed in quantity is the:
    (a)   Long run.
    (b)   Short run.
    (c)   Production run.
    (d)   Investment decision.

Problems and Applications

Exercise 1

In the text, an example of jeans production is used to show how many sewing machines and workers are needed per day to produce various quantities of jeans per day. A similar table is given here.

Table 5.1. The production of jeans (pairs per day)

Capital input (sewing machines per day)	Labor input (workers per day)							
	0	1	2	3	4	5	6	7
0	0	0	0	0	0	0	0	0
1	0	15	32	44	49	50	51	51
2	0	20	45	64	73	79	81	80

1. Suppose a firm had only two sewing machines and could vary only the amount of labor input. On the basis of Table 5.1, fill in column 2 of Table 5.2 to show how much can be produced at different levels of labor input when there are only two sewing machines.

Table 5.2. The production of jeans with two sewing machines

(1) Labor input (workers per day)	(2) Production of jeans (pairs per day)	(3) Marginal physical product (pairs per worker)
0	_____	_____
1	_____	_____
2	_____	_____
3	_____	_____
4	_____	_____
5	_____	_____
6	_____	_____
7	_____	_____

71

2. Graph the total output curve in Figure 5.1.

Figure 5.1

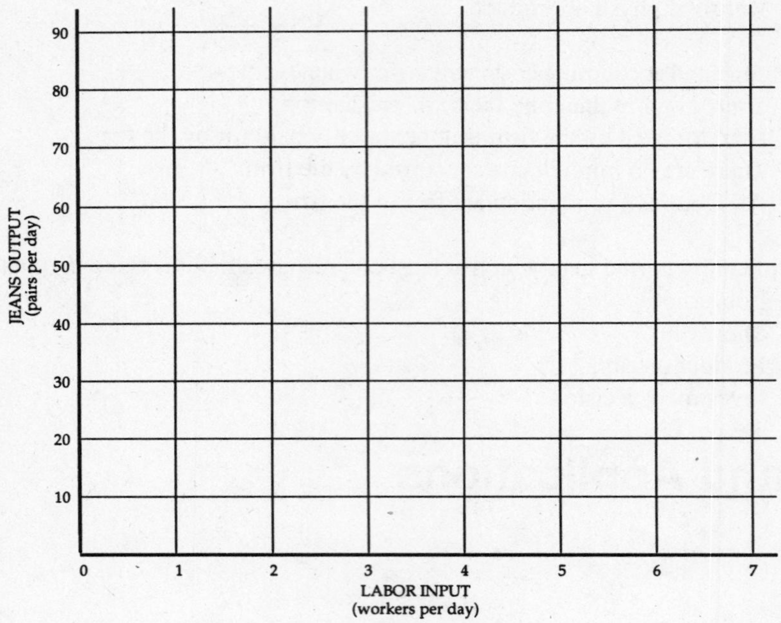

3. Compute the marginal physical product of each extra worker per day. Place the answers in column 3 of Table 5.2.

4. The law of diminishing returns states that the marginal physical product of a factor:
   (a) Will become negative as output increases.
   (b) Will decline as output increases.
   (c) Will increase and then decline as output increases.
   (d) Will begin to decline as more of the factor is used.

5. In Figure 5.1 at 3 units of labor, total output:
   (a) Is rising with increased labor usage.
   (b) Is falling with increased labor usage.
   (c) Remains constant with increased labor.

6. T   F   When marginal physical product declines, total output declines.

Exercise 2

This exercise shows the relationship between the various costs of production.

1. Complete Table 5.3 using the information given about output and the costs of production. (*Hint*: refer to Figure 5.3 and Figure 5.5 in the text if you need help getting started.)

72

Table 5.3 Costs of Production

Rate of Output	Fixed Cost	Variable Cost	Total Cost	Average Total Cost	Marginal Cost
0	$ _____	$ _____	$ 10	--------	-------
1	_____	6	_____	$ _____	$ _____
2	_____	10	_____	_____	_____
3	_____	16	_____	_____	_____
4	_____	_____	36	_____	_____
5	_____	40	_____	_____	_____
6	_____	_____	68	_____	_____

2. Graph marginal cost in Figure 5.2 and label it MC.

Figure 5.2

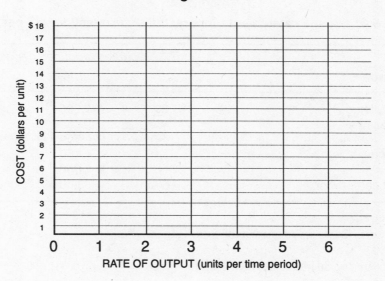

3. Graph the average total cost curve in Figure 5.2 and label it ATC. (Assume the ATC curve is equal to $8 at 3.5 units.)

4. When the average total cost curve is rising, the marginal cost curve is (above, below, equal to) the average total cost curve.

5. When the average total cost curve is falling, the marginal cost curve is (above, below, equal to) the average total cost curve.

6. When the average total cost curve is at its minimum, the marginal cost curve is (above, below, equal to) the average total cost curve.

Exercise 3

This exercise shows the relationship between fixed costs, variable costs, accounting cost, and economic cost. It is similar to Problem 4 in the text.

1. Fixed costs are defined as:
    (a) Costs that do not change with inflation.
    (b) Costs that are set firmly (without escalator clauses) in a contract.
    (c) Costs of production that do not change when the rate of production is altered.
    (d) Average costs that do not change when the rate of production is altered.

2. Variable costs include:
    (a) Costs of production that change when the rate of production is altered.
    (b) All costs in the long run.
    (c) The difference between total and fixed costs.
    (d) All of the above.

Table 5.4. Expense statement for parachute business (dollars per week)

Weekly expense	Parachutes produced per week		
	0	100	200
Lease on building	$1,200	$1,200	$1,200
Sewing machines	500	500	500
Nylon	0	300	700
Utilities (electricity, etc.)	0	150	200
Labor	0	650	650
Testing and certification	800	800	800

Use the information in Table 5.4 to answer the following questions.

3. Which items are considered to be fixed costs?

4. Calculate variable costs at an output level of 100 parachutes per week.

5. Calculate total costs at an output level of 100 parachutes per week.

6. Now assume the owner of the parachute business buys the building he is currently leasing so he no longer has a lease expenditure. Calculate the accounting cost at an output level of 200 parachutes per week.

7. Calculate the economic cost at an output level of 200 parachutes per week. Explain why there is a difference in the accounting cost at an output level of 200 parachutes and the economic cost.

Exercise 4

Reread the Headline article in the text entitled "Production and Investment Decisions." Then answer the following questions.

1. Which of the companies is making a production decision? How do you know?

2. Which of the companies is making an investment decision decision? How do you know?

Common Errors

The first statement in each "common error" below is incorrect. Each incorrect statement is followed by a corrected version and an explanation.

1. Total output starts falling when diminishing returns occur. WRONG!
   Diminishing returns set in when marginal physical product begins to decline. RIGHT!
   The law of diminishing returns describes what happens to *marginal physical product*, not total output. Marginal physical product will typically begin to decline long before total output begins to decline. For total output to decline, the marginal physical product must be negative.

2. The marginal cost curve rises because factor prices rise when more of a good is produced. WRONG!
   The marginal cost curve rises because the marginal productivity of the variable factor declines. RIGHT!
   The marginal cost curve moves in the opposite direction to the marginal physical product curve. Changes in factor prices would shift the whole marginal cost curve but would not explain its shape and would not affect the marginal physical product curve.

3. Marginal physical product begins to decline because inferior factors must be used to increase output. WRONG!
   Declining marginal physical product occurs even if all of the factors are of equal quality. RIGHT!
   Many people incorrectly attribute diminishing returns to the use of inferior factors of production. Diminishing returns result from an increasing ratio of the variable input to the fixed input. There is always a point where the variable input begins to have too little of the fixed input to work with. Result? Diminishing marginal product! The quality of the factors has nothing to do with it.

■ ANSWERS ■

Using Key Terms

Across

2. law of diminishing returns
3. production function
4. factors of production
8. fixed costs
11. profit
13. economic cost
14. supply
15. average total cost

Down

1. marginal physical product
3. production decision
5. investment decision
6. short run
7. marginal cost
9. total cost
10. variable costs
12. long run

True or False

1. F   The average producer earns a profit of approximately 4 to 6 percent.
2. F   A production function tells us the maximum output that can be produced with various combinations of factor inputs.
3. F   The company would be producing on the existing production function.
4. T
5. T
6. T
7. F   When output is zero in the short run, total costs are equal to fixed costs.
8. T
9. F   The ATC will not increase until the MC is greater than the ATC.
10. F   Economic costs exist whenever a factor of production is used to produce a good or service, whether or not an explicit payment is made, because other goods and services have to be given up.

Multiple Choice

1. c	5. b	9. a	13. a	17. d
2. c	6. d	10. c	14. d	18. b
3. d	7. a	11. a	15. c	19. b
4. d	8. b	12. d	16. c	20. a

Problems and Applications

Exercise 1

1. See Table 5.2 answer, column 2
3. See Table 5.2 answer, column 3.

Table 5.2 Answer

(1)	(2)	(3)
0	0	—
1	20	20
2	45	25
3	64	19
4	73	9
5	79	6
6	81	2
7	80	– 1

2. **Figure 5.1 Answer**

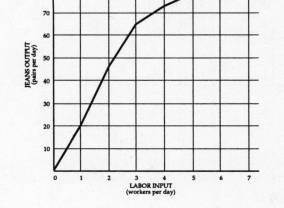

4. d
5. a
6. F   As long as marginal physical product is greater than zero total output increases.

Exercise 2

1. **Table 5.3 Answer**

Rate of Output	Fixed Cost	Variable Cost	Total Cost	Average Total Cost	Marginal Cost
0	$ 10	$ 0	$ 10	--------	-------
1	10	6	16	$ 16.00	$ 6
2	10	10	20	10.00	4
3	10	16	26	8.67	6
4	10	26	36	9.00	10
5	10	40	50	10.00	14
6	10	58	68	11.33	18

Figure 5.2 Answer

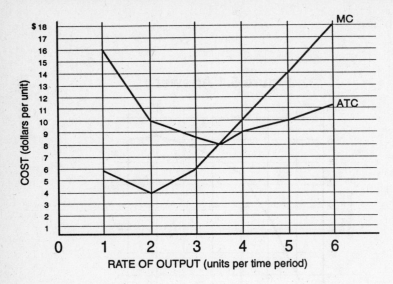

2. See the MC curve in Figure 5.2 answer.
3. See the ATC curve in Figure 5.2 answer.
4. Above
5. Below
6. Equal to

Exercise 3

1. c
2. d
3. Lease on the building, sewing machines, and testing and certification
4. $1,100
5. $3,600
6. $2,850
7. $4,050; The economic cost is greater because it includes the implicit cost of the building, the accounting cost does not.

CHAPTER 6

Competition

Quick Review

- Perfect competition is one of several market structures. Market structure affects the behavior of producers and influences market outcomes.

- A perfectly competitive firm cannot influence the price of its output and is referred to as a price taker. It is important to distinguish the firm's demand curve from the market-demand curve. The firm views its own demand curve as perfectly flat because it produces such a small part of market output, while the market demand curve is downward-sloping, reflecting the law of demand.

- In an effort to maximize profits, in the short run, a competitive firm will choose the rate of output where price equals marginal cost.

- A competitive firm's marginal cost curve above the average total cost curve is its short-run supply curve. The competitive market supply curve is the sum of the individual marginal cost curves.

- The determinants of supply include the price of inputs, technology, and expectations. If any of these determinants changes, the firm's supply curve will shift. Market supply will shift in response to a change in the supply curve of the individual firms or if the number of firms changes.

- The existence of short-term profits will encourage new firms to enter a competitive market. As they enter, the market supply will increase and push price down along the demand curve. Profit for the competitive firm will decrease.

- The limit to the competitive price and profit squeeze is reached when price is driven down to the level of minimum average total cost (ATC). If the market price falls below the minimum ATC, firms will exit from the industry. Price stabilizes when entry and exit cease. This long-run equilibrium occurs when economic profits reach zero.

- In competitive markets there is a persistent pressure on prices and profits. Firms must keep costs as low as possible by adopting the most efficient technologies. Competitive firms must also respond quickly to changes in demand by producing the goods and services demanded by buyers, in order to earn a profit. The penalty for not responding is losses and the potential failure of the firm.

Learning Objectives

After studying the chapter and doing the following exercises you should:

1. Know the elements that determine market structure.
2. Know the different types of market structure.
3. Be able to describe a competitive market.
4. Be able to explain why the demand curve faced by a competitive firm is flat.
5. Be able to distinguish the firm's demand curve from the market-demand curve.
6. Understand why competitive profit-maximization occurs where MC = Price.
7. Be able to graph the production decision and show the relevant profit and cost rectangles.
8. Understand why the marginal cost curve is the short-run supply curve for a competitive firm.
9. Be able to develop a competitive market supply curve.
10. Understand how economic profits and losses encourage entry and exit in competitive markets.
11. Be able to describe the sequence of events as a competitive market moves toward long-run equilibrium.
12. Understand why a competitive market promotes maximum efficiency.

Using Key Terms

Fill in the puzzle on the opposite page with the appropriate term from the list of Terms to Remember on page 148 in the text.

Across
2. The sole supplier of a good.
3. Determined by the intersection of the market demand curve and the market supply curve in Figure 6.2 in the text.
6. The goods and services that are given up when farmers choose to switch from growing crops to raising catfish.
8. The competitive _____ is summarized in Table 6.1 in the text.
9. The ability to alter the market price of a good or service.
10. Allows for indirect communication between producers and consumers by way of market sales and purchases.
15. The offer of goods at prices equal to their marginal cost.
16. Ranges from perfect competition to monopoly in Figure 6.1 in the text.

Down
1. This curve shifts to the right in Figure 6.8 in the text as the result of market entry.
4. Eventually becomes zero in a competitive industry because of market entry.
5. Equal to $52 at an output rate of four baskets per hour in Figure 6.4 in the text.
7. Not significant enough to prevent entry if a market is competitive.
8. The choice of a particular short-run rate of output by producers.
10. Equal to $5 at an output rate of one basket per hour in Figure 6.3 in the text.
11. This curve is the sum of the marginal cost curves of all the firms in a competitive industry.
12. An industry characterized by zero economic profit in the long run.
13. A firm that must take what ever price the market offers for the goods it produces.
14. Competitive markets promote _____ because the price of a good is driven down to its minimum average cost of production.

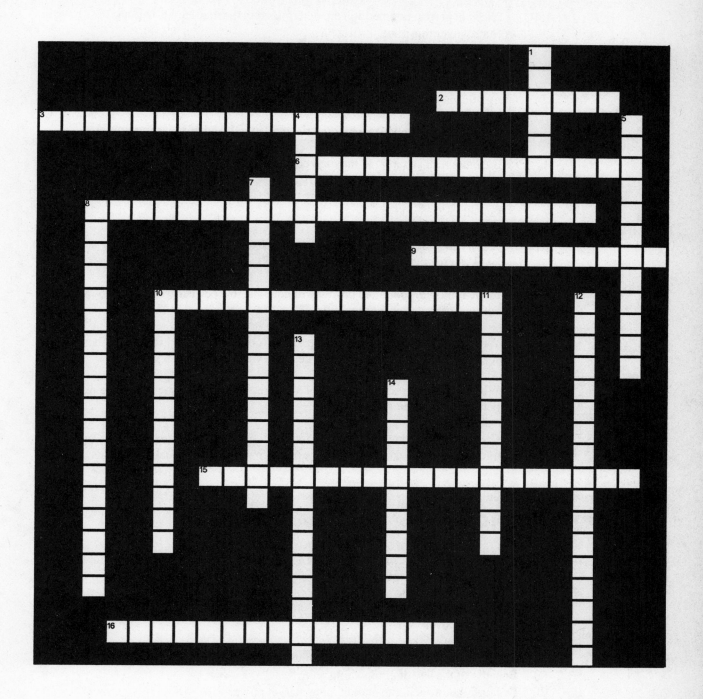

True or False: *Circle your choice and explain why any false statements are incorrect.*

T   F   1.   Prices in perfect competition are determined in the market; individual firms have no control over this price.

T   F   2.   If Farmer Betty (a farmer in the perfectly competitive tomato market) were to double her production of tomatoes, the market price and quantity of tomatoes would be significantly affected.

T   F   3.   In a perfectly competitive market, the market demand curve is horizontal.

T   F   4.   Business firms attempt to maximize total output.

T   F   5.   If a perfectly competitive firm were to raise its price above the market price, it would lose all its customers.

T   F   6.   A perfectly competitive firm will maximize total revenues by producing at an output level where price equals marginal cost (MC).

T   F   7.   In the long run, economic profits will not exist in a perfectly competitive market because of government regulation.

T   F   8.   When economic profits exist in a perfectly competitive market, the number of suppliers will increase and the market price will fall.

T   F   9.   When some firms are forced out of a market due to economic losses the result is a better use of our scarce resources.

T   F   10. Competitive markets provides society with the best answer to the WHAT to produce question because competitive firms produce where price equals marginal cost.

Multiple Choice: *Select the correct answer.*

_____   1.   Which of the following are characteristic of a perfectly competitive market structure?
  (a)   Many buyers and sellers.
  (b)   Low barriers to entry.
  (c)   Identical products.
  (d)   All of the above.

_____   2.   The market demand curve in a perfectly competitive market is downward sloping:
  (a)   Because of the law of diminishing returns.
  (b)   Because the firms in the market have market power.
  (c)   Because of the law of demand.
  (d)   All of the above.

3. If a perfectly competitive firm can sell 100 computers at $500 each, in order to sell one more computer, the firm:
   (a) Must lower its price.
   (b) Should raise its price.
   (c) Can sell the next computer for $500.
   (d) Cannot sell an additional computer at any price because the market is in equilibrium.

4. In which of the following types of markets does a single firm have the most market power.
   (a) Perfect competition.
   (b) Monopolistic competition.
   (c) Oligopoly.
   (d) Monopoly.

5. A perfectly competitive firm is a price taker because:
   (a) It has no control over the selling price of its product.
   (b) It has market power.
   (c) Market demand is downward sloping.
   (d) Its products are differentiated.

6. If a perfectly competitive firm wanted to maximize its total revenues, it would produce:
   (a) The output where MC equals price.
   (b) As much output as it is capable of producing.
   (c) The output where the ATC curve is at a minimum.
   (d) The output where the marginal cost curve is at a minimum.

7. The difference between the total cost and total revenue curves at a given output is:
   (a) Marginal cost.
   (b) Total profit.
   (c) Average total cost.
   (d) Average profit.

8. Refer to Figure 6.3 in the text. If the market price of catfish was $17 per basket, this farmer should produce:
   (a) Zero baskets.
   (b) Three baskets
   (c) Four baskets.
   (d) Five baskets.

9. Refer to Figure 6.4 in the text to help answer this question. If marginal cost exceeds price, a perfectly competitive firm can increase profits (or reduce losses) by:
   (a) Increasing output.
   (b) Raising the price.
   (c) Decreasing output.
   (d) Stopping production.

10. Refer to Figure 6.4 in the text to help answer this question. If price is greater than marginal cost, a perfectly competitive firm should increase output because:
    (a) Marginal cost is increasing.
    (b) Additional units of output add to the firm's profits (or reduce losses).
    (c) The price of the product is increasing.
    (d) Total revenue will increase.

11. Which of the following conditions always characterizes a firm that is maximizing profits in the short run?
    (a) Price equals minimum average total cost.
    (b) Price equals marginal cost.
    (c) There are no economic profits.
    (d) All of the above characterize such a firm.

12. Suppose that the cost of fertilizer decreases for peach farmers. In order to maximize profits, ceteris paribus, peach farmers should:
    (a) Decrease output.
    (b) Keep output the same since the market price did not change.
    (c) Increase output.
    (d) Increase price.

13. The market supply curve is calculated by:
    (a) Summing the marginal cost curves of all the firms.
    (b) Averaging the individual supply curves.
    (c) Summing the prices from individual supply curves.
    (d) Averaging individual marginal cost curves below ATC.

14. The market supply curve will shift due to all of the following except:
    (a) Changes in technology.
    (b) Changes in the number of supplying firms.
    (c) Changes in expectations about making profits in a market.
    (d) Changes in the current income of buyers.

15. A catfish farmer, in a perfectly competitive market,:
    (a) Is able to keep other potential catfish producers out of the market.
    (b) Would like to keep other potential catfish producers out of the market but cannot do so.
    (c) Will not care if more catfish producers enter the market.
    (d) Is powerless to alter his own rate of production.

16. In a perfectly competitive market with positive economic profits:
    (a) Firms will enter until economic profits are zero.
    (b) Firms will enter until accounting profits are zero.
    (c) Firms will exit until economic profits are zero.
    (d) No entry or exit will occur.

17. In a competitive market where firms are incurring losses, which of the following should be expected as the market moves to long-run equilibrium, *certeris paribus?*
    (a) A higher price and fewer firms.
    (b) A lower price and fewer firms.
    (c) A higher price and more firms.
    (d) A lower price and more firms.

18. In long-run competitive equilibrium, price equals:
    (a) Minimum average cost.
    (b) The point where MC intersects ATC.
    (c) The individual demand curve.
    (d) All of the above.

19. When economic losses exist in the potato chip market this is an indication that:
    (a) The goods and services that society is giving up are more valuable than the potato chips being produced.
    (b) Society's scarce resources are not being used in the best way.
    (c) Too many firms are producing potato chips (assuming that the market is perfectly competitive).
    (d) All of the above are correct.

20. In making a production decision, an entrepreneur:
    (a) Decides whether to enter or exit the market.
    (b) Makes a long-run decision about production.
    (c) Determines the short-run rate of output.
    (d) Determines plant and equipment.

Problems and Applications

Exercise 1

This exercise shows how the equilibrium price is determined in a competitive market and how the profit maximizing rate of output is determined in a perfectly competitive market.

1. Using the information in Table 6.1 draw the market demand curve for chicken eggs in Figure 6.1. Label the curve *D*. (Assume the demand curve is linear.)

Table 6.1. Market demand for eggs

Quantity (millions of eggs per day)	Price (per dozen)
2	$ 1.00
4	$ 0.50

Figure 6.1. Market demand and market supply curves

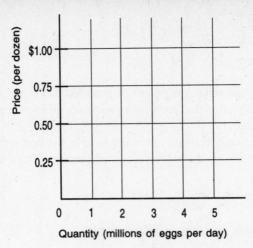

Quantity (millions of eggs per day)

2. Using the information in Table 6.2 draw the market supply curve for chicken eggs in Figure 6.1. Label the curve S. (Assume the supply curve is linear.)

Table 6.2. Market supply of eggs

Quantity (millions of eggs per day)	Price (per dozen)
4	$ 1.00
2	$ 0.50

3. Use the information in Table 6.3 to determine the marginal cost at each output level for an individual egg farmer.

Table 6.3. Production costs for an individual egg farmer

Quantity (eggs per minute)	Total cost	Marginal cost
0	$ 4.00	---------
1	$ 4.20	_____
2	$ 4.65	_____
3	$ 5.40	_____
4	$ 6.50	_____
5	$ 7.90	_____

86

4. Use the information in Table 6.3 to draw the marginal cost curve for the individual egg farmer in Figure 6.2.

Figure 6.2. Costs of egg production

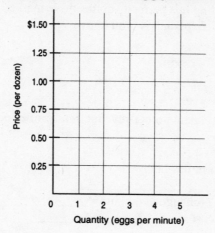

5. Use the market equilibrium price from Figure 6.1 to draw a line at the price that the individual farmer faces in Figure 6.2.

6. At an output level of 5 eggs per minute, for the individual farmer, MC is (greater, less) than price and the farmer should (increase, decrease) output in order to maximize profit.

Exercise 2

This exercise provides practice in using graphs in a perfectly competitive market situation.

1. Label the three curves given in Figure 6.3 for a firm in a perfectly competitive market situation.

Figure 6.3

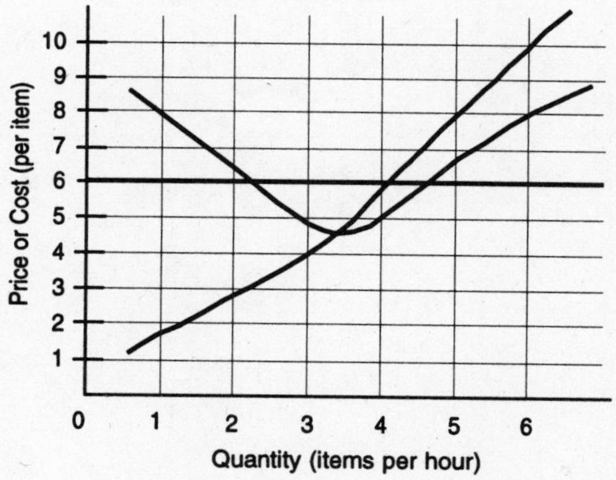

2. What is the profit maximizing rate of output for this firm?

3. Shade the area that represents total profit at the profit maximizing rate of output.

4. Given that the firm is operating in a perfectly competitive market, does this graph indicate a short-run or a long-run situation? Explain how you know.

Exercise 3

This exercise gives you a chance to calculate total revenue, total profit, and marginal cost and to find the output that will yield maximum profit.

1. Fill in the blanks for the formulas below.
   (a) Price x quantity = _____
   (b) (Change in total cost) / (change in output) = _____
   (c) Total revenue – total cost = _____

2. After checking your answers for Question 1, complete Table 6.4.

Table 6.4. Cost and revenue data

Qty.	Price	Total revenue	Total cost	Profit	Marginal cost
0	$7	$_____	$ 5.00	$_____	--------
1	7	_____	7.00	_____	_____
2	7	_____	11.00	_____	_____
3	7	_____	18.00	_____	_____
4	7	_____	27.00	_____	_____
5	7	_____	39.00	_____	_____

3. In Figure 6.4, graph price and marginal cost.

88

Figure 6.4

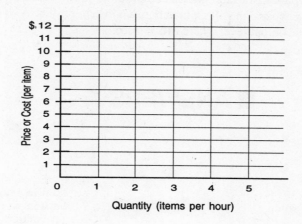

Quantity (items per hour)

4. What is the profit maximizing level of output for this firm?

5. At an output level of 4 items this firm would (increase, decrease) profit by producing more.

Common Errors

The first statement in each "common error" below is incorrect. Each incorrect statement is followed by a corrected version and an explanation.

1. The demand curve for a competitive market is flat. WRONG!
   The demand curve for a competitive firm is flat. RIGHT!
   > The error above results from failure to distinguish between the market and the firm.

2. Competitive firms do not make profits. WRONG!
   Competitive firms can make economic profits in the short run. RIGHT!
   > In the long run, firms enter a market and compete away economic profits. In the short run, a change in demand or supply may cause price to change and may allow a firm to earn temporary economic profits.

3. Since competitive firms make zero profits in the long run, they cannot pay their stockholders and they should shut down. WRONG!
   Since competitive firms make zero economic profits in the long run, they are able to pay all factors of production, including the skill of entrepreneurs, to keep the firms in existence. RIGHT!
   > **Be careful!** Keep the accounting and economic definitions of such words as "profit" separate and distinct. Keep movements along the supply curve (firms increase production rates) separate from shifts of the supply curve (firms enter or exit). Avoid confusing short-run responses (increasing production rates in existing plants) with long-run responses (entry or exit).

4. A firm should always increase the rate of production as long as it is making a profit. WRONG!
A profitable firm should increase production rates only as long as additional revenues from
the increase in production exceed the additional associated costs. RIGHT!

 If the increase in production rates generates more costs than revenue, the firm will be less profitable.
In this case, continued expansion will ultimately result in zero profits. A competitive firm will
maximize profits at the output level where MC = price.

■ ANSWERS ■

Using Key Terms

Across
2. monopoly
3. equilibrium price
6. opportunity cost
8. profit-maximization rule
9. market power
10. market mechanism
15. marginal cost pricing
16. market structure

Down
1. supply
4. profit
5. total revenue
7. barriers to entry
8. production decision
10. marginal cost
11. market supply
12. competitive market
13. competitive firm
14. efficiency

True or False

1. T
2. F   In a perfectly competitive market individual firms are so small relative to the market that any
change in a firm's price or output will have no impact on the market.
3. F   Market demand is downward sloping. The demand for one firm's product is horizontal.
4. F   Business firms attempt to maximize total profits.
5. T
6. F   The firm will maximize total profits at this output level.
7. F   Economic profits will not exist because additional firms will enter the market forcing prices
downward and economic profits to zero.
8. T
9. T
10. T

Multiple Choice

1. d	5. a	9. c	13. a	17. a
2. c	6. b	10. b	14. d	18. d
3. c	7. b	11. b	15. b	19. d
4. d	8. d	12. c	16. a	20. c

Problems and Applications

Exercise 1

Figure 6.1 Answer

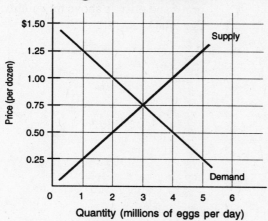

1. See Figure 6.1 answer.
2. See Figure 6.1 answer.

3. ### Table 6.3 Answer

Quantity	Marginal cost
0	---------
1	$ 0.20
2	0.45
3	0.75
4	1.10
5	1.40

Figure 6.2 Answer

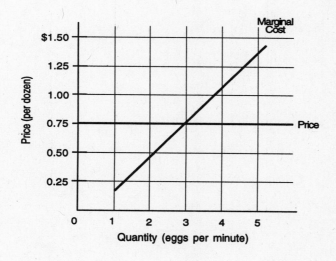

4. See Figure 6.2 answer.
5. See Figure 6.2 answer.
6. Greater, decrease

Exercise 2

1. **Figure 6.3 Answer**

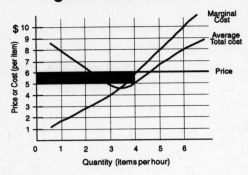

2. 4 items per hour.
3. See Figure 6.3 answer.
4. Short-run situation, because there is an economic profit and price is above the minimum of average total cost.

Exercise 3

1. a. total revenue
   b. marginal cost
   c. profit

2. **Table 6.4 Answer**

Quantity	Total revenue	Profit	Marginal cost
0	$ 0.00	$ − 5.00	-------
1	7.00	+ 0.00	$ 2.00
2	14.00	+ 3.00	4.00
3	21.00	+ 3.00	7.00
4	28.00	+ 1.00	9.00
5	35.00	− 4.00	12.00

3. **Figure 6.4 Answer**

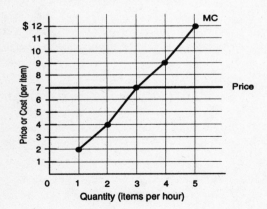

4. 3 items per day
5. Decrease

CHAPTER 7

Monopoly

Quick Review

- Monopoly is at the opposite end of the spectrum from perfect competition. A monopolist is the sole supplier in a given market and has market power with which it can influence price and output.

- The demand curve faced by a monopolist is the downward-sloping market demand curve. As a result, in order to sell more output a monopolist must lower its price, and the marginal revenue curve is always less than price.

- In making the production decision, monopolists attempt to maximize profits. They choose the rate of output at which marginal cost equals marginal revenue. When compared to the competitive producer, the monopolist will charge a higher price and will produce a smaller output.

- If market demand is sufficient, monopolists will reap economic profits that are a signal for other firms to enter the market. To maintain its status as the sole producer, the monopolist must be protected by some barrier to entry by competing firms. Barriers to entry take many forms including patents, legal harassment, exclusive licensing, bundled products, and government franchises.

- The existence of market power in the economy influences the answers we get to the WHAT, HOW, and FOR WHOM questions. By restricting output, the monopolist forces some resources to move where they will earn less and keeps economic profits for itself. Monopolists tend to be less efficient than competitive firms since they are not compelled by competitive forces to adopt the newest and most efficient technologies.

- Monopoly can sometimes be defended, however. It is argued that economic profits give the firm the financial resources, though perhaps not the incentive, to pursue research and development. Monopoly profits may also encourage entrepreneurial activity. In situations where economies of scale exist over the entire market, society will be best served by having a single firm (a "natural monopolist") produce all of the output. Some even argue that potential competition, perhaps from foreign producers attracted by economic profits, is sufficient to constrain the monopolist from exploiting its market power. In such "contestable markets" the economic outcomes may be more like that of the perfectly competitive market.

Learning Objectives

After studying the chapter and doing the following exercises, you should:

1. Understand the concept of market power and how it affects a firm or industry.
2. Understand that a monopolist faces the downward-sloping market demand curve and why marginal revenue is less than price.
3. Understand that the profit-maximizing rate of output for a monopolist occurs where marginal cost equals marginal revenue.
4. Know that a monopoly typically results in higher prices, lower output, and higher profits than would occur in a competitive market.
5. Understand the importance of barriers to entry for a monopoly and the different types of barriers.
6. Be able to compare and contrast the long run behavior of a competitive market vs. a monopoly.
7. Be able to describe the pros and cons of monopoly power.
8. Understand the concept of economies of scale and the occurance of natural monopoly.
9. Understand the idea and importance of "contestable markets."

Using Key Terms

Fill in the puzzle on the opposite page with the appropriate term from the list of Terms to Remember on page 168 in the text.

Across

1. For a monopolist this short-run choice is made by locating the intersection of marginal cost and marginal revenue.
2. An industry in which one firm can achieve economies of scale over the entire range of market supply.
4. Used to determine that the most profitable rate of production is four baskets per hour in Figure 7.2 in the text.
6. According to the article on page 160 in the text, the Justice Department was concerned that Microsoft Corporation had erected _____ by bundling products.
7. According to the article on page 159 in the text, Nintendo has used exclusive licensing to maintain its

   _____.
8. An imperfectly competitive industry which is restrained by potential competition.
9. This curve lies below the demand curve at every point except the first in Figure7.1 in the text.
11. A type of barrier to entry in which one large producer has an advantage over several smaller producers.

Down

1. Used to protect new inventions and acts as a barrier to entry.
3. The pricing method characteristic of competitive markets but not a monopoly.
5. Identical to the demand curve facing the firm in a monopoly situation.
10. The market structure that the member nations of OPEC are trying to duplicate in the article on page 162 in the text.

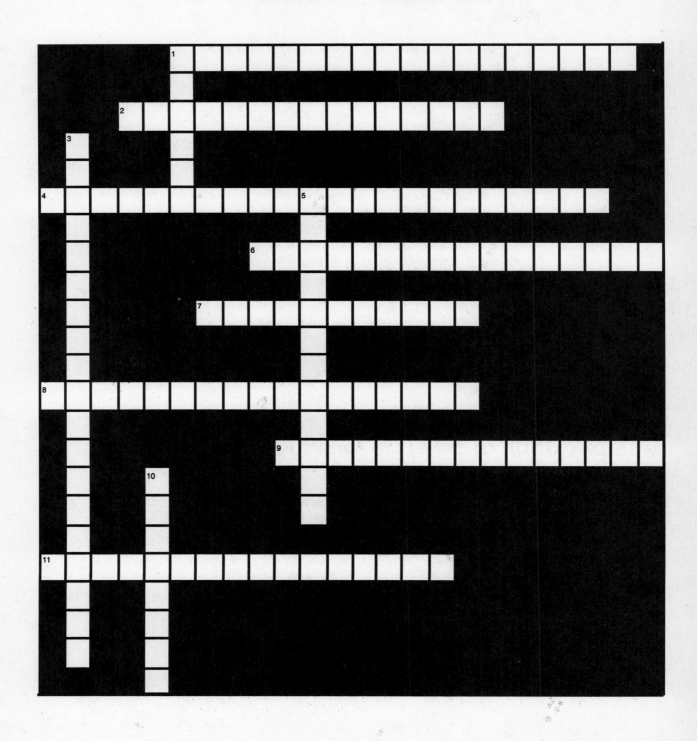

True or False: *Circle your choice and explain why any false statements are incorrect.*

T   F   1.   Since a monopoly firm controls the market, it can charge any price it wants and consumers will have to pay that price.

T   F   2.   Monopolists maximize profits at the output level where marginal cost equals marginal revenue.

T   F   3.   The demand for a monopolist's product is the same as the market demand for the product.

T   F   4.   The marginal revenue of a monopolist's product is less than the price because the monopolist faces a horizontal demand curve for its product.

T   F   5.   Since a monopolist is a price setter it will never experience economic losses in the short run.

T   F   6.   Patents, legal harassment, and product bundling are all examples of barriers to entry in monopoly markets.

T   F   7.   If a market changed from perfect competition to a monopoly, output would decrease and the price would increase, *ceteris paribus*.

T   F   8.   For both perfectly competitive and monopoly firms price exceeds marginal cost.

T   F   9.   A market that includes many firms with distinct brand images is referred to as perfect competition.

T   F   10.   Monopolies tend to inhibit technology and innovation by keeping competition out of the market.

Multiple Choice: *Select the correct answer.*

_____   1.   A firm has market power when:
    (a)   It faces a downward-sloping demand curve.
    (b)   It must lower its price to sell an additional unit of output.
    (c)   Its marginal revenue curve is below its demand curve.
    (d)   All of the above are correct.

_____   2.   Monopolists are:
    (a)   Price setters, but competitive firms are price takers.
    (b)   Price takers, as are competitive firms.
    (c)   Price takers, but competitive firms are price setters.
    (d)   Price setters, as are competitive firms.

3. For a monopolist, the demand curve facing the firm is:
   (a) The same as for the perfectly competitive firm.
   (b) The same as the market demand curve.
   (c) Always below marginal revenue.
   (d) A horizontal line.

4. The marginal revenue of a monopolist:
   (a) Is equal to price at all output levels.
   (b) Is below price.
   (c) Is constant up to the rate of output that maximizes total revenues.
   (d) Is the same as the market demand curve.

5. When a monopolist sells an additional unit of output, the marginal revenue will be lower than the price because:
   (a) The price of all the units sold will have to be lowered in order to sell the additional unit.
   (b) The monopolist faces a flat demand curve for its product.
   (c) Costs increase as more output is produced.
   (d) Economies of scale exist for monopolists.

6. Which of the following rules is always satisfied when any firm (i.e., perfectly competitive or monopoly) maximizes profit?
   (a) Price = lowest level of ATC.
   (b) Price = MC.
   (c) MR = MC.
   (d) Total revenue is also maximized.

7. The price charged by a profit-maximizing monopolist occurs:
   (a) At the minimum of the average total cost curve.
   (b) At the price where MR = MC.
   (c) At a price on the demand curve above the intersection where MR = MC.
   (d) At a price on the average total cost curve below the point where MR = MC.

8. In monopoly and perfect competition, a firm should expand production when:
   (a) Price is below marginal cost.
   (b) Price is above marginal cost.
   (c) Marginal revenue is below marginal cost.
   (d) Marginal revenue is above marginal cost.

9. When a monopoly continues to make above-normal profits in the long run, you can be sure that:
   (a) It produces more efficiently than a competitive market can.
   (b) Barriers to entry prevent other firms from competing away the above-normal profits.
   (c) There is a conspiracy between the government and the monopolist to maintain high prices.
   (d) It has a flat demand curve, which gives it greater revenue.

10. Which of the following is not a barrier to entry into a monopoly market?
    (a) Economies of scale.
    (b) Bundling products.
    (c) Legal harassment.
    (d) Monopoly profits.

11. In Figure 7.3 in the text, a competitive industry will have an incentive to produce more than 4 baskets per hour because:
    (a) The MC is above the ATC.
    (b) The MR is greater than the MC.
    (c) The demand is greater than the MC.
    (d) Demand is above the ATC.

12. In the Headline article about Microsoft on page 160 in the text, which of the following practices is Microsoft accused of using to limit competition?
    (a) The threat of legal action.
    (b) Exclusive licensing.
    (c) Bundling products.
    (d) Government franchises.

13. A monopoly realizes larger profits than would occur in a comparable competitive market by:
    (a) Setting a higher price at the competitive level of output, thereby increasing total revenue.
    (b) Producing a greater quantity at the competitive price, thereby increasing profits.
    (c) Producing at output levels with a more favorable cost structure and charging the competitive market price, thereby increasing profits per unit.
    (d) Reducing production and pushing price up.

14. A monopolist is typically able to enjoy economic profits in the long run because of:
    (a) Barriers to entry.
    (b) The monopolist's ability to set prices.
    (c) Economies of scale.
    (d) The monopolist's ability to sell as much as it produces at the market price.

15. Suppose that a market is dominated by three firms. This type of market is known as:
    (a) Perfect competition.
    (b) A monopoly.
    (c) Monopolistic competition.
    (d) An oligopoly.

16. Monopoly might be considered to be more desirable than perfect competition because:
    (a) The monopolist has more incentive to keep costs down.
    (b) Monopoly is the best way of increasing output above the competitive level of production.
    (c) Marginal revenue is less than price for a monopoly.
    (d) Economies of scale can only be fully realized by a single firm in a natural monopoly.

17. Which of the following is an accurate argument in support of market power?
    (a) It increases output and raises price, contributing to greater consumption of scarce resources.
    (b) Monopoly profits can provide incentives to pursue research and development.
    (c) It contributes to efficient production when there are diseconomies of scale.
    (d) It provides the economic profit necessary for survival and efficient production in a market.

_____ 18. Economies of scale:
(a) Allow many small firms to expand society's production possibilities.
(b) Continue no matter how large the firm becomes.
(c) Occur any time a firm produces more.
(d) Can be a convincing argument for allowing a monopoly to exist.

_____ 19. Which of the following is the unique characteristic of natural monopolies that other monopolies do not experience?
(a) Economies of scale occur over the entire range of market output.
(b) The marginal cost curve is always above the average total cost curve.
(c) The profit-maximizing rate of output occurs where MC equals price.
(d) The characteristics are the same because all monopolies are natural monopolies.

_____ 20. Contestable market theory focuses on:
(a) Vigorous price rivalry.
(b) Government regulation.
(c) Potential entry.
(d) All of the above.

Problems and Applications

Exercise 1

This exercise provides practice in calculating total revenue and marginal revenue and shows the relationship between marginal revenue and demand.

1. Use the information given in Table 7.1 to calculate total revenue and marginal revenue.

Table 7.1. Revenue data

	Quantity	Price	Total Revenue	Marginal Revenue
A	0	$ 12.00	$_____	-------
B	1	11.00	_____	$ _____
C	2	10.00	_____	_____
D	3	9.00	_____	_____
E	4	8.00	_____	_____
F	5	7.00	_____	_____
G	6	6.00	_____	_____

2. Use the information from Table 7.1 to graph the demand curve and the marginal revenue curve in Figure 7.1. Label each curve and label the points (*B* through *G*) on the demand curve.

Figure 7.1. Demand and marginal revenue curves

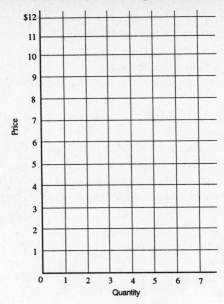

Exercise 2

This exercise reviews costs and revenues and provides further experience with profit maximization.

1. Figure 7.2 represents cost curves for a monopolist. Label the average total cost curve, the marginal cost curve, the marginal revenue curve, and the demand curve in Figure 7.2.

Figure 7.2. Cost curves and profit maximization

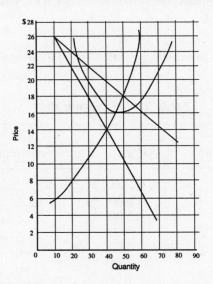

2. What is the profit-maximizing rate of output for the monopolist in Figure 7.2?

3. What price will the monopolist charge in Figure 7.2?

4. Shade the area to indicate total profit for the monopolist at the profit-maximizing rate of output in Figure 7.2?

5. Now assume the curves in Figure 7.2 represent a competitive industry. What are the profit-maximizing rate of output and price? How do they compare to the profit-maximizing rate of output and price for a monopolist?

Exercise 3

Reread the Headline article entitled "Barriers to Entry" on page 159 in the text.

1. What phrase indicates that Nintendo Co. has successfully exploited monopoly power in the video game market?

2. What barriers to entry kept other firms from competing with Nintendo and sharing in the profits available in the market?

Common Errors

The first statement in each "common error" below is incorrect. Each incorrect statement is followed by a corrected version and an explanation.

1. The shaded area in Figure 7.3a shows total profit. WRONG!

Figure 7.3a

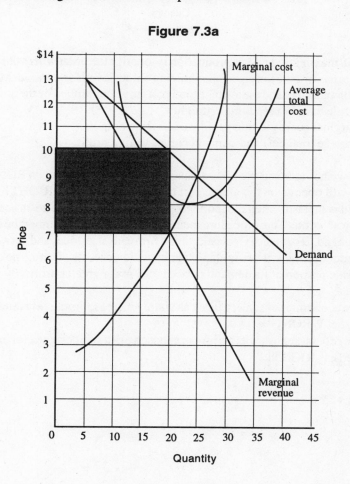

The shaded area in Figure 7.3b shows total profit. RIGHT!

Figure 7.3b

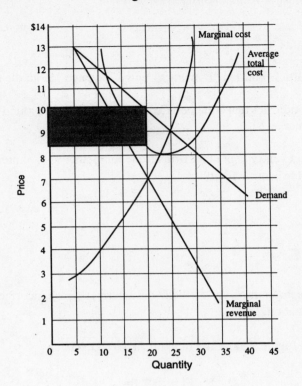

The profit-maximizing rate of production is found at the point where the MR curve intersects the MC curve. But *after* finding the profit-maximizing output level, forget about MR = MC. The difference between the demand curve and the average total cost curve, multiplied by the quantity, equals total profit.

Here's a rule to help keep things straight:
- Use marginal curves to find profit-maximizing output.
- Use average total cost and demand curves to find profit.

2. A monopolist wishes to be on the inelastic part of the demand curve. WRONG!
A monopolist will operate on the elastic part of the demand curve. RIGHT!

If demand is inelastic, then the monopoly can usually decrease costs and increase revenues by cutting back production. This procedure means more profits. Remember the total-revenue test for the elasticity of demand. If demand is inelastic, then a firm can raise prices and get more revenues. Of course, with lower production rates, the firm also experiences lower costs. There is no doubt about it, if any firm is on the inelastic portion of its demand curve, it can make greater profits by raising prices!

3. When there are economies of scale, a firm can simply increase production rates in the short run and unit costs will decline. WRONG!
When there are economies of scale, a firm can choose a plant size designed for increased production rates at lower unit costs. RIGHT!

102

Economies of scale are not realized through production decisions in the short run. They are realized through investment decisions, by the choice of an optimal-sized plant for higher production rates. Scale refers to plant size or capacity, not to production rates within a plant of a given size. Think of economies of scale in terms of investment decisions concerning choices of optimal capacity for the long run, not production decisions concerning the lowest cost production in the short run.

■ ANSWERS ■

Using Key Terms

Across
1. production decision
2. natural monopoly
4. profit-maximization rule
6. barriers to entry
7. market power
8. contestable market
9. marginal revenue
11. economies of scale

Down
1. patent
3. marginal cost pricing
5. market demand
10. monopoly

True or False

1. F   The demand for a monopolist's product is typically not perfectly inelastic. The monopolist is constrained by the consumer's willingness and ability to purchase their product.
2. T
3. T
4. F   The marginal revenue of a monopolist's product is less than the price because the monopolist must lower its price to sell more of its product.
5. F   The monopolist's ability to raise prices is limited by consumer demand. If the price the monopolist charges is less than the ATC, losses will exist.
6. T
7. T
8. F   For perfectly competitive firms price equals marginal cost, but for a monopolist price exceeds marginal cost.
9. F   Such a market is referred to as monopolistic competition.
10. T

Multiple Choice

1. d	5. a	9. b	13. d	17. b
2. a	6. c	10. d	14. a	18. d
3. b	7. c	11. c	15. d	19. a
4. b	8. d	12. c	16. d	20. c

Problems and Applications

Exercise 1

1. Table 7.1 Answer

Quantity	Total revenue	Marginal revenue
0	$ 0.00	-----
1	11.00	$ 11.00
2	20.00	9.00
3	27.00	7.00
4	32.00	5.00
5	35.00	3.00
6	36.00	1.00

2. Figure 7.1 Answer

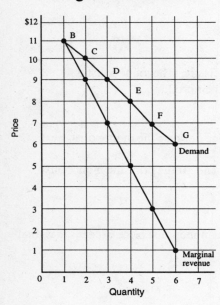

Exercise 2

1. **Figure 7.2 Answer**

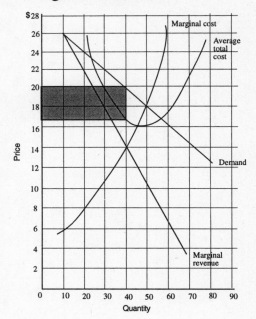

2. 40 units
3. $20 per unit
4. See Figure 7.2 answer
5. 50 units at $18 per unit, the price is lower and the output is greater.

Exercise 3

1. "…forecast profits of $1.2 billion this fiscal year for Nintendo." These profits apparently vaulted Nintendo into the rank of other Japanese powerhouses.

2. The barrier to entry is the control of the technology required to produce and play the games.

CHAPTER 8

The Labor Market

Quick Review

- The motivation to work springs from a variety of social, psychological, and economic forces. The need to have income to purchase desired goods and services is, of course, very important. Working imposes opportunity costs on the worker because leisure time must be given up when one chooses to work.

- The individual's supply curve of labor slopes upward and to the right because of increasing opportunity costs and the decreasing marginal utility of income. The market supply of labor shows the total quantity of labor that workers are willing and able to supply at alternative wage rates in a given time period, *ceteris paribus*.

- The demand for labor is derived from the demand for the goods and services it is used to produce. The quantity of labor demanded will increase as the wage rate decreases. The marginal physical produce (MPP) of labor is the addition to total output because of an additional worker. The demand curve for labor is the marginal revenue product (MRP) curve; it combines laborers' productivity with the price of the output. The law of diminishing returns affects both MPP and MRP.

- The hiring decision requires that managers take account of labor's contribution to the firm's revenues (called its marginal revenue product) and what it costs to hire the labor. The marginal revenue product thus sets an upper limit to the wage which will be paid to labor. Labor should be hired until the marginal revenue product declines to the level of the wage rate. Both increases in labor's productivity and increases in the market price of the output will shift the demand for labor (MRP curve) to the right.

- The market equilibrium wage is determined by the intersection of the market supply and market demand curves. A minimum wage is set above the market equilibrium wage and causes the quantity of labor supplied to exceed the quantity of labor demanded. Unemployment is the inevitable result. Labor unions must exclude some workers from the market to achieve their goals, and the displaced workers depress wages in other markets.

- It is sometimes difficult to determine the wages of certain individuals because their marginal revenue product is so difficult to calculate. In this situation opportunity wages, custom, power, tradition, and the like are used to determine the wage.

Learning Objectives

After studying the chapter and doing the following exercises you should:

1. Understand the tradeoff between income and leisure.
2. Be able to apply the law of diminishing marginal utility to the labor-supply decision.
3. Be able to explain and draw the individual supply curve and the market supply curve for labor.
4. Understand that the demand for labor is a derived demand.
5. Understand the concepts of marginal physical product and marginal revenue product and how they are both affected by the law of diminishing returns.
6. Know the relationship between marginal revenue product and labor demand and how the hiring decision is made.
7. Understand how market supply and market demand determine the equilibrium wage rate and the level of employment.
8. Understand the impact of a change in productivity and a change in output price.
9. Be able to demonstrate the impact of minimum-wage policies and describe how unions influence the labor market.
10. Know when to apply the concept of the "opportunity wage" in explaining wage levels and wage differentials.

Using Key Terms

Fill in the puzzle on the opposite page with the appropriate term from the list of Terms to Remember on page 190 in the text.

Across

2. The downward-sloping curve in Figure 8.7 in the text.
7. The curve pictured in Figure 8.1 in the text.
8. Determined by the intersection of the two curves in Figure 8.5 in the text.
10. Equal to five boxes per hour when George is hired as the second strawberry picker in Figure 8.3 in the text.

Down

1. Explains why the marginal physical product of labor declines as the quantity of labor increases.
3. Used to justify the compensation given to Disney's CEO in the article on page 188 in the text.
4. Equal to $4 when five strawberry pickers are hired in Table 8.1 in the text.
5. The total quantity of hours people are willing and able to work at various wages.
6. The demand for labor that results from the demand for final goods and services.
9. The _____ of working is the leisure time that must be given up.

Puzzle 8.1

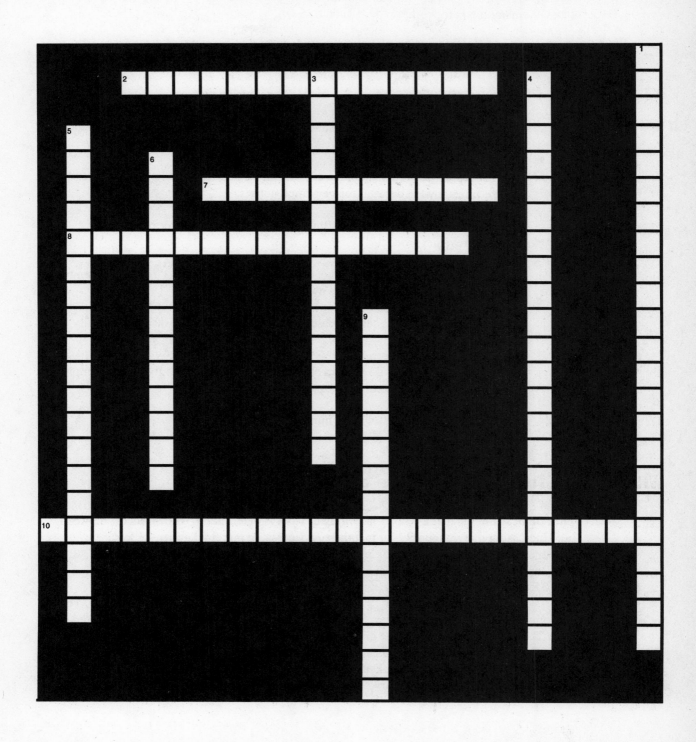

True or False: *Circle your choice and explain why any false statements are incorrect.*

T   F   1.   People are only concerned with maximizing their income when determining how many hours to work.

T   F   2.   The supply of labor is upward sloping because of the law of diminishing marginal returns.

T   F   3.   The marginal utility of income decreases as total income increases.

T   F   4.   The market supply of labor is the summation of all the quantities of labor demanded by businesses at each wage rate.

T   F   5.   The concept of derived demand means that the demand for bricklayers, for example, is determined by the demand for new brick houses.

T   F   6.   The highest wage that a firm is willing to pay its workers is determined by the marginal revenue product.

T   F   7.   If a firm's marginal physical product curve slopes downward, its marginal revenue product curve must also slope downward.

T   F   8.   The only way that wages can increase without sacrificing jobs is for productivity to increase.

T   F   9.   The demand for labor is downward sloping because as the quantity of labor employed increases, the workers become less qualified.

T   F   10.   All workers are better off when a minimum wage is imposed.

Multiple Choice: *Select the correct answer.*

_____ 1.   The number of hours that a worker is willing to work is determined by the tradeoff between:
   (a)   Increasing marginal utility for income and decreasing marginal utility for leisure.
   (b)   Increasing marginal utility for leisure and decreasing marginal utility for income.
   (c)   Increasing total utility for leisure and decreasing total utility for income.
   (d)   Decreasing total utility for leisure and increasing total utility for income.

_____ 2.   The opportunity cost of working is:
   (a)   The leisure time that must be given up.
   (b)   The wages that the worker must give up by not working additional hours.
   (c)   The financial cost to the worker of driving to work, parking, buying lunch, etc.
   (d)   The amount of utility the worker receives when working.

3. Which of the following is a reason why workers typically require higher wages in order to work additional hours?
   (a) The increasing opportunity cost of labor.
   (b) The increasing value of leisure time forgone.
   (c) The law of diminishing marginal utility applied to additional income.
   (d) All of the above are correct.

4. If consumers wanted to increase wages and the number of jobs available for apple pickers, the best strategy would be to:
   (a) Insist that the government establish a minimum wage for apple pickers.
   (b) Boycott apples until wages increased.
   (c) Buy more apples.
   (d) Insist that the sellers raise the price of apples.

5. A firm's demand for labor is downward sloping (i.e., additional workers are worth less to employers) because:
   (a) Total output decreases as more workers are hired.
   (b) The firm must raise wages to hire more workers.
   (c) The marginal physical product of labor decreases as more labor is hired.
   (d) The price of the product declines as the firm produces and sells more.

6. The marginal physical product (MPP) of labor decreases as more labor is hired because of:
   (a) The law of diminishing returns.
   (b) A decrease in total output.
   (c) A decrease in the skills of the additional workers hired.
   (d) The law of diminishing marginal utility.

7. In order to calculate marginal revenue product, we need to know:
   (a) The marginal revenue and the cost of the factor.
   (b) The marginal physical product and the unit price of the factor.
   (c) The marginal revenue and the amount of the product produced.
   (d) The marginal physical product and the price of the product.

8. The marginal revenue product curve and marginal physical product curve have similar shapes:
   (a) Because marginal revenue product depends on marginal physical product.
   (b) Because the product demand curve slopes downward in accordance with the law of diminishing returns.
   (c) Because the law of diminishing marginal utility and the law of diminishing returns are due to the same economic behavior.
   (d) For all the above reasons.

9. Refer to Figure 8.3 in the text. The effect of the law of diminishing returns is not evident in Figure 8.3 until the _____ worker is hired.
   (a) First
   (b) Third
   (c) Fifth
   (d) Eighth

10. A firm should continue to hire workers until:
    (a) The MRP is equal to demand.
    (b) The MPP is equal to the market wage rate.
    (c) The MRP is equal to the market wage rate.
    (d) The MRP is equal to zero.

11. Refer to Table 8.2 in the text. If strawberry pickers worked for zero wages (i.e., they were volunteers), how many workers should this firm hire?
    (a) Zero.
    (b) Two, where MRP is at a maximum.
    (c) Seven, where MRP is zero.
    (d) Nine, or as many as possible.

12. Refer to Figure 8.4 in the text. At a wage rate of $4 per hour, this firm would *not* hire the sixth worker because:
    (a) The value of the sixth worker's production is less than $4.
    (b) Total production begins to decline.
    (c) MPP begins to decline.
    (d) The price of strawberries will begin to decline at this level of production.

13. The University of Florida football coach discussed in the text gets paid nine times more than the University's president because:
    (a) The coach is more popular.
    (b) The coach has a higher level of education.
    (c) The coach has been employed at the university longer than the president.
    (d) The coach brings more revenue to the university than the president.

14. Which of the following is true about the equilibrium market wage?
    (a) All workers are satisfied with the wage.
    (b) All employers are satisfied with the wage.
    (c) There is no unemployment in this market at the equilibrium wage.
    (d) All of the above are correct.

15. Employment will definitely rise when:
    (a) Productivity and wages both rise.
    (b) Productivity rises and wages fall.
    (c) Productivity falls and wages rise.
    (d) Productivity and wages both fall.

16. What will happen to wages and the level of employment when there is a reduction in the size of the labor force, *ceteris paribus*?
    (a) Wages will rise but employment will fall.
    (b) Wages will fall but employment will rise.
    (c) Both wages and employment will fall.
    (d) Both wages and employment will rise.

17. What will happen to wages and the level of employment in a market when the government eliminates a minimum wage, *ceteris paribus*?
    (a) Wages will rise but employment will fall.
    (b) Wages will fall but employment will rise.
    (c) Both wages and employment will fall.
    (d) Both wages and employment will rise.

18. To maintain above-equilibrium wages, unions use which of the following forms of exclusion?
    (a) Union membership.
    (b) Required apprenticeship programs.
    (c) Employment agreements negotiated with employers.
    (d) All of the above.

19. The effect of union exclusion on nonunion workers is to:
    (a) Cause a shortage of nonunion workers.
    (b) Lower the wages of nonunion workers.
    (c) Increase the number of jobs for nonunion workers.
    (d) All of the above.

20. When a worker's MRP is difficult to measure, for example, a college professor or corporate CEO, wages can be determined by:
    (a) The supply of labor alone.
    (b) The minimum wage.
    (c) The wages the worker would receive in his or her best alternative job.
    (d) The average wage of government workers.

Problems and Applications

Exercise 1

This exercise illustrates the relationship between marginal physical product and marginal revenue product for a company producing bottled water.

1. T F The marginal physical product (MPP) measures the change in total output that occurs when one additional worker is hired.

2. Which of the following formulas would provide a correct calculation of the marginal physical product? (The symbol Δ refers to a change in a variable, q refers to output, and L refers to quantity of labor.)
    (a) q / L
    (b) $\Delta q / L$
    (c) $\Delta q / \Delta L$
    (d) $\Delta TR / \Delta L$

3. Calculate total revenue, marginal revenue product, and marginal physical product for Table 8.1.

Table 8.1. Marginal physical product and marginal revenue product

(1) Labor (workers per hour)	(2) Quantity produced (gallons per hour)	(3) Price (dollars per gallon)	(4) Total revenue (dollars per hour)	(5) Marginal revenue product (dollars per worker)	(6) Marginal physical product (gallons per worker)
0	0	$1	_____	_____	_____
1	15	1	_____	_____	_____
2	27	1	_____	_____	_____
3	36	1	_____	_____	_____
4	42	1	_____	_____	_____
5	45	1	_____	_____	_____
6	46	1	_____	_____	_____

4. The law of diminishing returns implies that:
   (a) The marginal revenue declines as additional labor is employed in a given production process.
   (b) The marginal revenue product declines as additional labor is employed in a given production process.
   (c) The marginal physical product of labor increases as additional labor is employed in a given production process.
   (d) None of the above.

5. T F There are diminishing returns to labor with increased production in Table 8.1.

Exercise 2

This exercise provides experience in computing and graphing derived demand as well as determining the number of workers to hire.

1. You are a producer of Rotgut Ripple, which sells for $2 per gallon. In its desire to lend some local color to your country, the government permits you to produce it in the hills. It is hard to get people to work for you. You have to pay $6 an hour for labor. Complete Table 8.2.

114

Table 8.2. Rotgut Ripple production, by labor hours

(1) Wage (dollars per hour)	(2) Labor (workers per hour)	(3) Quantity produced (gallons per hour)	(4) Price (dollars per gallon)	(5) Total revenue (dollars per gallon)	(6) Marginal revenue product (dollars per worker)
6	0	0	$1	$_____	$ _____
6	1	15	1	_____	_____
6	2	27	1	_____	_____
6	3	36	1	_____	_____
6	4	42	1	_____	_____
6	5	45	1	_____	_____
6	6	46	1	_____	_____

2. T   F   The demand curve for Ripple workers is found by plotting the marginal revenue product curve.

3. In Figure 8.1 draw the demand curve for labor. Label it demand or MRP.

Figure 8.1

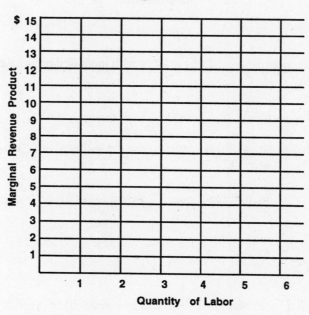

4. Draw a straight line at a wage of $6 in Figure 8.1 and label it wage rate.

5. How many workers are you willing to hire to produce Rotgut Ripple? _____

6. How many gallons of Ripple will be produced per hour? _____

Exercise 3

This exercise examines the impact of a minimum wage on a labor market.

1. Figure 8.2 shows the labor market for unskilled workers. The equilibrium wage rate occurs at $ _____ per hour and at a quantity of _____ workers.

Figure 8.2

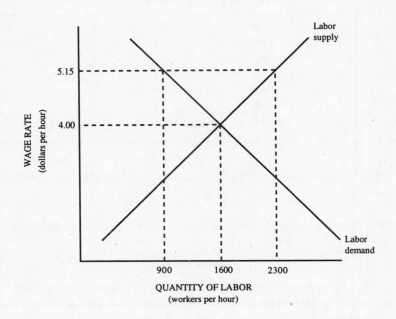

2. Now assume that a minimum wage is set at $5.15 per hour. The result of this government intervention is to create a (shortage, surplus) of labor.

3. At the new minimum wage _____ workers keep their jobs and _____ workers lose their jobs.

4. According to the article on page 186 in the text, why does President Clinton believe an increase in the minimum wage is important?

5. An increase in labor productivity in Figure 8.2 would cause the labor (supply, demand) curve to shift to the (left, right).

Common Errors

The first statement in each "common error" below is incorrect. Each incorrect statement is followed by a corrected version and an explanation.

1. Workers demand jobs. WRONG!
   Employers demand labor services and workers (employees) supply them. RIGHT!

   Demand refers to what a buyer is willing and able to buy. Certainly workers are not seeking to pay their employers. Rather, the workers are trying to find someone who is willing and able to pay them for their labor.

2. Employers employ those factors that are least expensive. WRONG!
    Employers want to employ those factors that are most cost-effective. RIGHT!

    If a factor is cheap, there may be a reason. It may not last long, may not work correctly, or may require heavier use of other factors of production—for example, maintenance workers. The marginal productivity of the cheap factor may therefore be low. An apparently more expensive factor might perform its proper function well and even save on the costs of other factors. The marginal productivity of the more expensive input would more than make up for its higher cost. Businesses would choose the more expensive factor of production.

3. Marginal revenue product is the same as marginal revenue. WRONG!
    The marginal revenue product curve applies to the factor market while the marginal revenue curve applies to the product market. RIGHT!

    The formula for marginal revenue product is:

$$\frac{\text{Change in total revenue}}{\text{Change in quantity of input}}$$

while that for marginal revenue is:

$$\frac{\text{Change in total revenue}}{\text{Change in quantity of output}}$$

Marginal revenue shows changes in total revenue due to increased output and therefore is appropriate in analyzing what happens in the product market. Marginal revenue product shows changes in total revenue due to the increased use of a factor and therefore is appropriate in analyzing what happens in the factor market. Both curves are derived from the demand curve in the product market. However, in order to find marginal revenue product, it is also necessary to know the relationship between the quantity of input and quantity of output. That is why the marginal physical product becomes important.

■ ANSWERS ■

Using Key Terms

Across
2. demand for labor
7. labor supply
8. equilibrium wage
10. marginal physical product

Down
1. law of diminishing returns
3. opportunity wage
4. marginal revenue product
5. market supply of labor
6. derived demand
9. opportunity cost

True or False

1. F Workers attempt to achieve a balance between more income and more leisure time.
2. F The supply of labor is upward sloping because workers must be compensated with higher wages in order to give up additional leisure.
3. T
4. F The market supply of labor is the summation of all the quantities of labor supplied by workers at each wage rate.
5. T
6. T
7. T

8. F An increase in the demand for the product being produced can also cause wages to increase without sacrificing jobs.
9. F The demand for labor is downward sloping because as the quantity of labor employed increases, the less capital and space additional workers have to work with and MPP declines.
10. F The workers that are able to find a job will be better off but fewer workers will be hired.

Multiple Choice

1. b	5. c	9. b	13. d	17. b
2. a	6. a	10. c	14. c	18. d
3. d	7. d	11. c	15. b	19. b
4. c	8. a	12. a	16. a	20. c

Problems and Applications

Exercise 1

1. T
2. c
3. **Table 8.1 Answer**

(1) Labor	(4) Total revenue	(5) Marginal revenue product	(6) Marginal physical product
0	----	----	----
1	$15	$15	15
2	27	12	12
3	36	9	9
4	42	6	6
5	45	3	3
6	46	1	1

4. b
5. T

Exercise 2

1. **Table 8. 2 Answer**

(2) Labor	(5) Total revenue	(6) Marginal revenue product
0	$ 0	$ ----
1	15	15
2	27	12
3	36	9
4	42	6
5	45	3
6	46	1

2. T

118

3. **Figure 8.1 Answer**

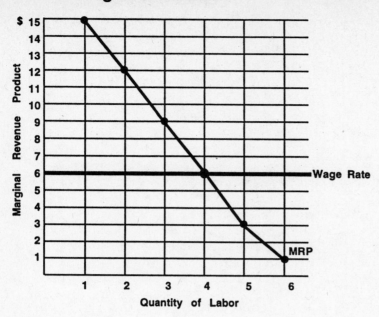

Quantity of Labor

4. See Figure 8.1 answer.
5. 4
6. 42

Exercise 3

1. $4.00; 1600
2. shortage
3. 900; 700
4. "...to help families coming off welfare."
5. Demand, right

CHAPTER 9

Government Intervention

Quick Review

- Market failure occurs when the market mechanism causes the economy to produce a combination of goods different from the optimal mix of output or results in an inequitable distribution of income. Market failure may prompt the government to intervene.

- There are four specific sources of market failure: public goods, externalities, market power, and equity.

- Public goods are those that cannot be consumed exclusively, like private goods. Public goods, like national defense, are consumed jointly by all of us no matter who pays. Because the link between paying and receiving is broken, everyone seeks to be a "free rider" and benefit from purchases made by others. As a result, no one demands public goods in the marketplace. Some level of government must then provide these goods.

- Externalities are costs (or benefits) of a market transaction borne by a third party. Externalities create a divergence between social costs and private costs and lead to suboptimal market outcomes. In the case of externalities such as pollution (which imposes costs on society), too much of the polluting good is produced. If the externality produces benefits, too little of the good will be produced by the market alone. Regulations and emission fees are used to reduce the external costs associated with externalities.

- Market power allows producers to ignore the signals generated in the marketplace and produce a suboptimal mix of output. Antitrust policy and laws seek to prevent or restrict concentrations of market power.

- The market mechanism tends to allocate output to those with the most income. The government has responded by providing transfer payments to ensure a more equitable distribution of income and output.

- Markets may also fail at the macro level. The problems here show up in unacceptable levels of unemployment, inflation, and economic growth. Government intervention is then necessary to achieve society's goals.

- Government intervention that does not improve economic outcomes is referred to as government failure.

Learning Objectives

After studying the chapter and doing the following exercises, you should:

1. Understand the nature and causes of market failure.
2. Be able to describe the communal nature of public goods and the free-rider dilemma.
3. Know the nature of externalities and how they influence decision making on the part of producers and consumers.
4. Use the concepts of social cost and private cost to explain the problems associated with externalities.
5. Understand the basic policy options that can be used to address the problems associated with externalities.
6. Understand how antitrust activity attempts to combat monopoly power.
7. Be familiar with some fundamental antitrust laws.
8. Understand that inequity in income distribution is an example of market failure with respect to the FOR WHOM question.
9. Understand the concepts of macro failure and government failure.

Using Key Terms

Fill in the puzzle on the opposite page with the appropriate term from the list of Terms to Remember on page 211 in the text.

Across

3. Can be consumed jointly.
5. The ability to alter the market price of a good or service.
6. The costs of an economic activity incurred directly by the producer.
7. One who does not pay but still enjoys the benefits.
10. The likely outcome of government intervention according to the survey on page xxx in the text.
11. Exceed private costs by the amount of external costs.
12. For a _____, consumption by one person excludes consumption by others.
13. Referred to as the "invisible hand."
14. A form of government intervention to address the FOR WHOM question.

Down

1. The legislation used to break up monopolies such as AT&T.
2. Labeled as point X in Figure 9.1 in the text.
4. Represented by point M in Figure 9.1 in the text.
8. A type of market failure discussed in the article on page 198 in the text.
9. Used to close the gap between marginal social costs and marginal private costs in Figure 9.5 in the text.

Puzzle 9.1

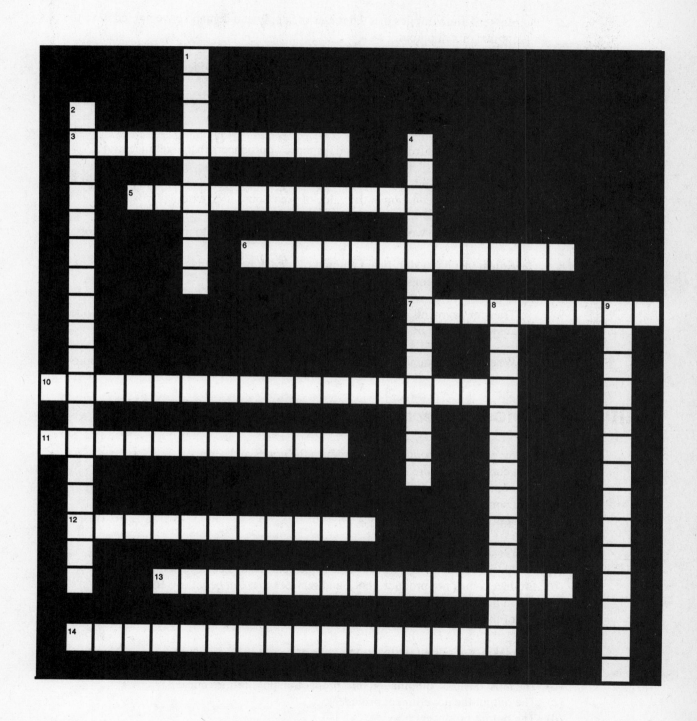

True or False: *Circle your choice and explain why any false statements are incorrect.*

T   F   1.   Any combination of goods and services on the production-possibilities curve can be considered an optimal mix.

T   F   2.   Market failure implies that the forces of supply and demand have not led us to the optimal mix of output.

T   F   3.   The term public good refers to any good or service provided by the government.

T   F   4.   The free-rider dilemma refers to a situation in which a consumer can consume a good or service without having to pay for it.

T   F   5.   Pollution results from the flawed response of producers to market incentives.

T   F   6.   If a neighbor paints his house a bright purple and, as a result, the value of your house decreases, the reduction in the value of your house is an externality.

T   F   7.   An emission fee would shift marginal social costs closer to marginal private costs.

T   F   8.   A firm that has a significant amount of market power tends to produce more of their product than is considered optimal.

T   F   9.   Transfer payments are a government response to the market's failure to provide a fair answer to the FOR WHOM question.

T   F   10.   When the government responds to a market failure, outcomes will always improve.

Multiple Choice: *Select the correct answer.*

_____   1.   In a market economy, producers will produce the goods and services:
    (a) That consumers desire the most.
    (b) That consumers need the most.
    (c) That consumers demand.
    (d) That optimize consumer utility.

_____   2.   The market sometimes fails to produce society's optimum output because:
    (a) Producers do not always measure the same benefits and costs as society.
    (b) Producers may not produce goods and services that can be jointly consumed.
    (c) When producers have market power, they tend to underproduce goods and services.
    (d) All of the above are correct.

_____   3.   The optimal mix of output is always the same as:
    (a) The output consumers demand.
    (b) The most desired combination on a production possibilities curve.
    (c) The output the government provides.
    (d) The output producers provide.

4. Governments usually build highways because it is difficult to exclude people who don't pay for the highways from using them. What type of market failure is most likely involved?
   (a) Inequity.
   (b) Public goods.
   (c) Government failure.
   (d) Market power.

5. In economics, a public good:
   (a) Is any good produced by the government.
   (b) Has social costs of production that are lower than private costs of production.
   (c) Is provided in an optimal amount by the market.
   (d) Cannot be denied to consumers who do not pay.

6. A private good:
   (a) Can be enjoyed exclusively by the one who pays for the good.
   (b) Experiences free riders.
   (c) Results in market failure when provided in markets characterized by laissez-faire.
   (d) Is provided most efficiently by government.

7. When external costs result from the production of a good:
   (a) Producers have an incentive to produce too little.
   (b) Consumers have an incentive to consume too little.
   (c) Both producers and consumers have an incentive to produce and consume too much.
   (d) Producers and consumers are not affected.

8. The market will overproduce goods that have external costs because:
   (a) Producers experience lower costs than society.
   (b) Producers experience higher costs than society.
   (c) The government is not able to produce these goods.
   (d) Producers cannot keep these goods from consumers who do not pay so they have to produce greater amounts.

9. Social costs:
   (a) Are less than private costs.
   (b) Include private costs.
   (c) Are unrelated to private costs.
   (d) Do not affect society.

10. Internalizing the costs of pollution by establishing emission charges can cause:
    (a) An upward shift in the polluting firm's MC curve.
    (b) An upward shift in the polluting firm's ATC curve.
    (c) A reduction in the polluting firm's output.
    (d) All of the above.

11. Which type of market failure is addressed in the article entitled "Passive Smoke Deadly" on page 198 in the text?
    (a) The failure to produce public goods.
    (b) External costs.
    (c) Market power by cigarette producers.
    (d) Inequity in the distribution of goods.

12. The cost of environmental protection can be measured by:
    (a) The difference between social benefits and social costs.
    (b) The difference between marginal social benefits and marginal social costs.
    (c) The opportunity cost of resources used to protect the environment.
    (d) The dollar damage caused by pollution.

13. Refer to Figure 9.5 in the text. A completely successful emission fee would:
    (a) Shift the private MC curve so that the curve intersects with price at zero output, that is, pollution is completely eliminated.
    (b) Shift the private MC curve to the same position as the social MC curve.
    (c) Shift the social MC curve to the same position as the private MC curve.
    (d) Not shift either the private or social MC curve.

14. What type of market failure provided the justification for breaking up AT&T?
    (a) Market power.
    (b) Public goods.
    (c) Externalities.
    (d) Inequity.

15. The development of market power by a firm is considered to be a market failure because firms with market power:
    (a) Produce more and charge a lower price than what is socially optimal.
    (b) Tend to ignore external costs.
    (c) Produce less and charge a higher price than what is socially optimal.
    (d) Do not respond to consumer demand.

16. The first antitrust act to prohibit "conspiracies in restraint of trade" was:
    (a) The Sherman Act.
    (b) The Clayton Act.
    (c) The Federal Trade Commission Act.
    (d) Case decisions such as those involving AT&T and IBM.

17. The federal government's role in transfer payment programs is justified by considerations of:
    (a) Equity.
    (b) Public goods and externalities.
    (c) Market power.
    (d) Macro failure.

18. If government involvement forces the economy inside the production-possibilities curve, then there is:
    (a) Government failure.
    (b) Waste.
    (c) Inefficiency.
    (d) All of the above.

19. A source of government failure that is *not* generally an example of market failure includes:
    (a) Monopoly.
    (b) Externalities.
    (c) Inequity.
    (d) Waste.

_____ 20. When macro failures of the market occur, government intervention is justified because:
   (a) The economy is not producing on the production-possibilities curve.
   (b) Price levels are not stable.
   (c) Economic growth is considered to be too slow.
   (d) All of the above could be reasons for macro intervention.

Problems and Applications

Exercise 1

Assume point *A* represents the optimal mix of output in Figure 9.1. Determine which letter best represents the following situations. Then answer Questions 4-7.

Figure 9.1

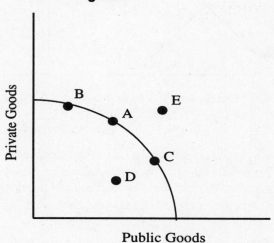

Public Goods

_____ 1. Government failure at the micro level that results in an overproduction of public goods.

_____ 2. The free-rider dilemma.

_____ 3. Macro instability.

4. The market mechanism tends to _____ private goods and _____ public goods.

5. In terms of the production-possibilities curve, _____ failures imply that society is at the wrong point on the curve and _____ failures imply that society is inside the curve.

6. Market failures justify government _____.

7. If government involvement fails to improve market outcomes then there is _____.

127

Exercise 2

This exercise shows how externalities affect third parties.

A chemical plant and a plastics factory are located adjacent to the same stream. The chemical plant is located upstream. The downstream plastics factory requires pure water for its production process. Its basic supply is the stream that runs past both firms.

Figure 9.2

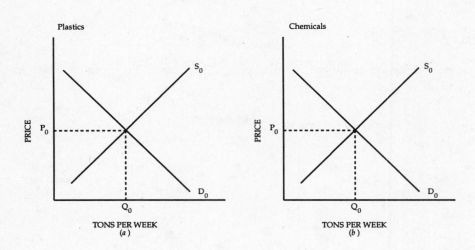

In Figure 9.2a and b, S_0 and D_0 represent the supply and demand for plastics and chemicals, respectively. Assume that the economy is initially competitive and resources are allocated efficiently. Equilibrium price and quantity are P_0 and Q_0 in each case. But then the chemical producer decides to dump waste products into the stream rather than dispose of them with the costly process that had been used.

1. In Figure 9.2b draw a new supply curve for chemicals after the dumping in the stream begins. Label it S_1. (There are many ways to draw this curve correctly.)

2. The pollution from the chemical plant forces the plastics manufacturer to use a costly water-purifying system. Draw a new supply curve for plastics in Figure 9.2a. Label it S_1. (There are many ways to draw this curve correctly.)

3. The effect of pollution on the quantity of chemicals sold is the same as if:
    (a) A new, improved technology were discovered.
    (b) Wages to its labor force were reduced.
    (c) The Social Security tax on employers had been abolished.
    (d) All of the above were the case.

128

4. As a result of the chemical plant's polluting activities:
   (a) The price of chemicals has risen.
   (b) The price of chemicals has fallen.
   (c) The price of plastics has not changed.
   (d) None of the above is the case.

5. As a result of the chemical plant's activities:
   (a) More chemicals are produced and sold than society desires.
   (b) More labor is used to produce chemicals than society desires.
   (c) More capital inputs are used to produce chemicals than society desires.
   (d) All of the above are the case.

6. The effect of the chemical firm's pollution is to:
   (a) Raise the price of plastics and reduce the quantity sold.
   (b) Lower the price of plastics and increase the quantity sold.
   (c) Raise the price of plastics and increase the quantity sold.
   (d) Do none of the above.

7. The impact of the pollution on the plastics industry in this example is to:
   (a) Reduce the output of plastics below the level that society desires.
   (b) Reduce the employment possibilities in the plastics industry.
   (c) Raise the price of products made with plastics.
   (d) Do all of the above.

Exercise 3

This exercise shows the difference between private marginal costs and social marginal costs.

1. An iron-producing firm generates pollution as it mines iron ore. Assume the iron ore market is competitive. Table 9.1 depicts the private costs and social costs of the firm's iron production at each daily production rate. Complete Table 9.1.

Table 9.1. Costs of producing iron

Production rate (tons per day)	Total private cost (dollars per day)	Private marginal cost (dollars per ton)	Total social cost (dollars per day)	Social marginal cost (dollars per ton)
0	$ 0	$ ---	$ 0	$ ---
1	40	_____	80	_____
2	90	_____	170	_____
3	150	_____	270	_____
4	220	_____	380	_____
5	300	_____	500	_____
6	390	_____	630	_____
7	490	_____	770	_____
8	600	_____	920	_____
9	720	_____	1,080	_____
10	850	_____	1,250	_____
11	990	_____	1,430	_____
12	1,140	_____	1,620	_____

2. In Figure 9.3 the price of the iron in the market is $140 per ton. Draw the marginal revenue curve and label it MR. Draw the private marginal cost curve and label it PMC. Draw the social marginal cost curve and label it SMC.

Figure 9.3

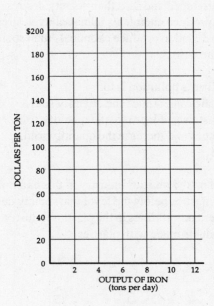

3. What is the profit-maximizing production rate for the firm if it considers only its private costs?
   (a) 5 tons per day.
   (b) 7 tons per day.
   (c) 9 tons per day.
   (d) 11 tons per day.

4. What is the profit-maximizing production rate if the firm is required to pay all social costs?
   (a) 5 tons per day.
   (b) 7 tons per day.
   (c) 9 tons per day.
   (d) 11 tons per day.

5. How much should the pollution (emission) fee be to induce the iron-producing firm to produce the socially optimal rate of output?
   (a) $2 per ton.
   (b) $20 per ton.
   (c) $40 per ton.
   (d) $100 per ton.

130

Common Errors

The first statement in each "common error" below is incorrect. Each incorrect statement is followed by a corrected version and an explanation.

1. Fire protection, police protection, education, and other services can be produced more efficiently by the private sector than by the public sector. WRONG!
   The public sector can produce many services more efficiently than the private sector. RIGHT!
   You should recognize now that the existence of externalities and the free-rider dilemma force society to produce some goods and services through public-sector expenditures. Many of the goods and services we take for granted (such as education) would not be produced in sufficient quantities if left to the private sector. And can you imagine trying to provide for your own defense against foreign countries?

2. Public goods can be produced only by government. WRONG!
   Public goods can be produced by government or the private sector. RIGHT!
   Whether a good is a public good or not does not depend on whether it is produced in the public or private sector. Public goods are those that are consumed jointly, by both those who pay and those who don't. All things produced or done by government are not public goods. Frequently a fee will be charged to use a government facility or program, thus creating a link between paying and using.

■ ANSWERS ■

Using Key Terms

Across
3. public good
5. market power
6. private costs
7. free rider
10. government failure
11. social costs
12. private good
13. market mechanism
14. transfer payments

Down
1. antitrust
2. optimal mix of output
4. market failure
8. externalities
9. emission charge

True or False

1. F To be considered optimal, a combination of goods and services must be the best single point on the production-possibilities curve.
2. T
3. F The term public good refers to those goods and services that cannot be consumed exclusively, that is, those who do not pay cannot be excluded from the benefits.
4. T
5. F Pollution results from the rational response by producers to market incentives. The problem is in the market signals, not the response.
6. T
7. F An emission fee would shift marginal private costs closer to marginal social costs by raising the costs of production.
8. F A firm that has a significant amount of market power will tend to produce less of their product than would be considered optimal.
9. T
10. F Government intervention can result in an outcome that is worse than the market outcome. This is referred to as government failure.

Multiple Choice

1. c	5. d	9. b	13. b	17. a
2. d	6. a	10. d	14. a	18. d
3. b	7. c	11. b	15. c	19. d
4. b	8. a	12. c	16. a	20. d

Problems and Applications

Exercise 1

1. c
2. b
3. d
4. Overproduce, underproduce
5. Micro, macro
6. Intervention
7. Government failure

Exercise 2

1. **Figure 9.2 Answer**

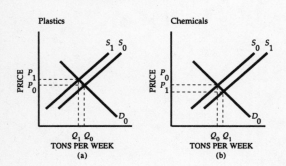

TONS PER WEEK
(a)

TONS PER WEEK
(b)

2. See Figure 9.2 answer (a), line S_1.
3. d
4. b
5. d
6. a
7. d

132

Exercise 3

1. **Table 9.1 Answer**

Production rate	Private marginal cost	Social marginal cost
0	$ —	$ —
1	40	80
2	50	90
3	60	100
4	70	110
5	80	120
6	90	130
7	100	140
8	110	150
9	120	160
10	130	170
11	140	180
12	150	190

2. **Figure 9.3 Answer**

3. d
4. b
5. c

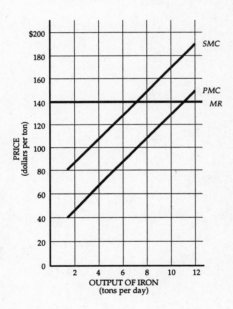

133

CHAPTER 10

The Business Cycle

Quick Review

- Business cycles are alternating periods of growth and contraction in the economy. The cycle is measured by changes in the nation's real GDP. The cycles vary in length and intensity. The worst contraction experienced was the Great Depression of the 1930s. Despite the ups and downs, the economy has had an average annual growth rate of approximately 3 percent since 1929.

- Macroeconomic theory attempts to explain the business cycle while macroeconomic policy tries to control the cycle.

- A recession is accompanied by a higher unemployment rate for the labor force. To be counted as part of the labor force you must be over 16 and be employed or actively seeking employment. The unemployment rate is calculated by dividing the number of unemployed by the total labor force.

- Economists acknowledge four different types of unemployment. Seasonal unemployment is related to the seasons of the year. Frictional unemployment is typically short in duration and is related to the job search. Structural unemployment is caused by a mismatch between the skills of the applicants and the requirements of the available jobs. Cyclical unemployment occurs when the economy does not create enough jobs. The full employment goal is the lowest rate of unemployment that still allows for price stability.

- Inflation is an increase in the average level of prices of goods and services. Inflation acts like a tax, taking from some and giving to others, because prices do not rise at the same rate for the various combinations of goods and assets that people buy and sell.

- Inflation creates uncertainty for all of the decision makers in the economy—households, business, and government.

- Inflation is typically measured using the Consumer Price Index (CPI), a weighted average of prices paid by consumers at the retail level. The inflation rate is the percentage change in the CPI from one year to the next. The goal for price stability is an inflation rate of less than 3 percent, which reduces the conflict with full employment and allows for quality improvements.

Learning Objectives

After studying the chapter and doing the following excercises you should:

1. Understand how the business cycle is measured.
2. Have a historical perspective on the business cycle from the Great Depression to the present.
3. Be able to calculate and interpret the unemployment rate.
4. Be able to categorize the unemployed into seasonal, frictional, cyclical, and structural categories.
5. Be able to explain the "full employment rate of unemployment" as a policy goal.
6. Understand the difference between a change in average prices and relative prices and how inflation is defined.
7. Be able to explain how inflation redistributes income and wealth based on the price, income, and wealth effects.
8. Understand how inflation creates uncertainty for decision makers in the economy.
9. Understand that the CPI is a measure of weighted average prices and be able to calculate the annual rate of inflation.
10. Understand why the full employment and price stability goals are not zero.

Using Key Terms

Fill in the puzzle on the opposite page with the appropriate term from the list of Terms to Remember on page 236 in the text.

Across

6. A decrease in average prices.
7. The number of unemployed people divided by the size of the labor force.
8. The price of apples compared to the price of other fruit.
10. Decreases for college students as tuition increases, *ceteris paribus*, according to the article on page 228 in the text.
12. Approximately 6.7 million Americans were included in this statistic in 1997 according to Figure 10.3 in the text.
13. Alternating periods of economic activity shown in Figure 10.1 in the text.
15. Income received in a given time period measured in current dollars.
16. An economic situation that has occurred twelve times since 1929 according to Table 10.1 in the text.

Down

1. Computed by the Bureau of Labor Statistics as the average price of consumer goods.
2. The lowest rate of unemployment compatible with price stability.
3. Established at a rate of less than 3 percent inflation in the Full Employment and Balanced Growth Act of 1978.
4. Results in a redistribution of income and wealth.
5. The increase in the average price level over a particular time period.
9. The study of aggregate economic behavior.
11. Included approximately 138 million Americans in 1997 according to Figure 10.3 in the text.
14. Used to measure economic growth in Figure 10.2 in the text.

Puzzle 10.1

True or False: *Circle your choice and explain why any false statements are incorrect.*

(T) F 1. A business cycle indicates the change in real GDP in an economy over time.

T (F) 2. The production of goods and services in the U.S. has risen steadily since 1929.

T (F) 3. During the business cycle, unemployment and production typically move in the same direction.

T (F) 4. A person who quits one job to take another after a short vacation is not considered to be unemployed.

(T) F 5. Cyclical unemployment is the result of insufficient demand in the economy for goods and services.

T (F) 6. Full employment means that everyone in the labor force has a job.

(T) F 7. During periods of inflation some prices may actually fall.

T (F) 8. Everyone is made worse off during periods of inflation.

(T) F 9. When nominal incomes increase at a slower rate than the rate of inflation, real incomes decrease.

(T) F 10. If all prices and wages in the economy rose by the same percentage during the same time period, inflation would not cause a redistribution of income.

Multiple Choice: *Select the correct answer.*

_____ A 1. The growth and contraction in the production of goods and services over time define:
   (a) The business cycle.
   (b) Unemployment.
   (c) Inflation.
   (d) Macro policy.

_____ B 2. Business cycles in the United States:
   (a) Are similar in length but vary greatly in magnitude.
   (b) Vary greatly in length, frequency, and magnitude.
   (c) Are similar in frequency, and magnitude.
   (d) Are similar in length, frequency, and magnitude.

_C_   3. A downturn in the business cycle is characterized by:
  (a) Lower unemployment rates.
  (b) Higher prices.
  (c) Lower real output.
  (d) Higher interest rates.

_A_   4. Real GDP serves as a better measure of the health of the economy than nominal GDP because real GDP adjusts for:
  (a) Changes in the price level.
  (b) Changes in production.
  (c) Changes in the price level and production.
  (d) The production by factors located outside of the U.S.

_A_   5. The labor force is smaller than the total population because the labor force does not include:
  (a) The very young and old.
  (b) People who have jobs.
  (c) People looking for a job.
  (d) Those who are unhappy with the job they have.

_B_   6. Which of the following would be counted as a member of the labor force?
  (a) A housewife that works 12 hours a day taking care of her children, cleaning her house, etc.
  (b) An unemployed steelworker actively looking for employment.
  (c) A student attending college.
  (d) A retired member of the armed forces collecting a pension.

_B_   7. Which of the following would be counted as unemployed?
  (a) Amy, who is on vacation but will soon return to the same job.
  (b) Bob, a college student looking for summer work.
  (c) Carol, who is on welfare.
  (d) Dave, who is on strike.

_D_   8. Our full employment goal is not zero percent because:
  (a) Frictional unemployment will always exist.
  (b) Unacceptably high rates of inflation would probably result.
  (c) There will always be the kinds of changes in the economy that cause structural unemployment.
  (d) All of the above are reasons.

_D_   9. Which of the following unemployment categories is most clearly related to the rate of growth of real GDP?
  (a) Structural.
  (b) Seasonal.
  (c) Frictional.
  (d) Cyclical.

_C_   10. Which of the following situations characterizes frictional unemployment when other forms of unemployment are low?
  (a) There are not enough jobs for those experiencing frictional unemployment.
  (b) Those who experience frictional unemployment cannot perform the jobs available.
  (c) The period of job search will be relatively short.
  (d) All of the above.

_A_   11. Automobile workers in Detroit who are unemployed because of foreign automobile imports at the same time that job vacancies exist for coal miners in West Virginia would most likely be classified as:
(a) Structurally unemployed.
(b) Cyclically unemployed.
(c) Frictionally unemployed.
(d) Seasonally unemployed.

_D_   12. Refer to the Headline article on page 221 in the text. Which of the following workers would probably *not* qualify for unemployment benefits?
(a) A worker who quits his or her job.
(b) A college professor during the summer.
(c) A worker who works for one month and is laid off.
(d) None of these workers are likely to qualify for benefits.

_D_   13. Which of the following could occur during periods of inflation?
(a) Some prices could fall.
(b) People that have borrowed money could gain.
(c) The real incomes of some people could fall.
(d) All of the above could occur during periods of inflation.

_B_   14. If the number of dollars you receive every year is the same, but prices are rising, then your nominal income:
(a) Rises and your real income rises.
(b) Stays the same but your real income falls.
(c) Rises but your real income falls.
(d) Falls but your real income rises.

_A_   15. Comparing changes in relative prices is more useful than examining changes in average prices when:
(a) Determining the redistribution of income due to inflation.
(b) Determining the inflation rate.
(c) Calculating the CPI.
(d) Determining the deflation rate.

_D_   16. Changes in relative prices may occur during periods of:
(a) Inflation.
(b) Stable prices.
(c) Deflation.
(d) All of the above.

_B_   17. Inflation acts like a tax because:
(a) The government tends to benefit during periods of inflation.
(b) It takes purchasing power from some people and gives it to others.
(c) Inflation pushes everyone into higher tax brackets.
(d) Everyone loses purchasing power during periods of inflation just like everyone pays taxes.

_C_ 18. Jane Dough's nominal annual income in 1998 was $40,000. Suppose that during the 1998-2000 period the total rate of inflation was ten percent. To keep Jane's real income constant, her nominal income in the year 2000 should be:
(a) $40,000.
(b) $4,000.
(c) $44,000.
(d) $80,000.

_C_ 19. If the Consumer Price Index (CPI) had a value of 120 in 1998, this means that during the period between the base year and 1998:
(a) All prices increased by 20 percent.
(b) Prices of goods and services that producers buy increased by an average of 20 percent.
(c) Prices of goods and services that the typical consumer buys increased by an average of 20 percent.
(d) All prices increased by an average of 120 percent.

 20. The CPI tends to overestimate the rate of inflation because:
(a) Only the goods and services that consumers buy are included in the calculation.
(b) Some price increases are an indication of higher quality products.
(c) The CPI measures changes in average prices, not changes in relative prices.
(d) Some price increases are simply the result of greedy producers and sellers.

Problems and Applications

Exercise 1

This exercise shows how to calculate the unemployment rate and indicates the relationship between the unemployment rate and GDP.

1. Compute the unemployment rate based on the information in Table 10.1, and insert it in column 4.

Table 10.1. Unemployment and real GDP, 1980–94

Year	(1) Noninstitutional population	(2) Civilian labor force (thousands of persons 16 and over)	(3) Unemployment (thousands of persons 16 and over)	(4) Unemployment rate (percent)	(5) Percentage change in real GDP
1981	170,130	108,670	8,273	_____	2.5
1982	172,271	110,204	10,678	_____	−2.1
1983	174,215	111,550	10,717	_____	4.0
1984	176,383	113,544	8,539	_____	6.8
1985	178,206	115,461	8,312	_____	3.7
1986	180,587	117,834	8,237	_____	3.0
1987	182,753	119,865	7,425	_____	2.9
1988	184,613	121,669	6,701	_____	3.8
1989	186,393	123,869	6,528	_____	3.4
1990	188,049	124,787	6,874	_____	1.3
1991	189,765	125,303	8,426	_____	−1.0
1992	191,576	126,982	9,384	_____	2.7
1993	193,550	128,040	8,734	_____	2.2
1994	196,814	131,056	7,996	_____	3.5
1995	198,584	132,304	7,404	_____	2.0

2. In Figure 10.1 graph both the unemployment rate (column 4 of Table 10.1) and the percentage change in real GDP (column 5).

Figure 10.1

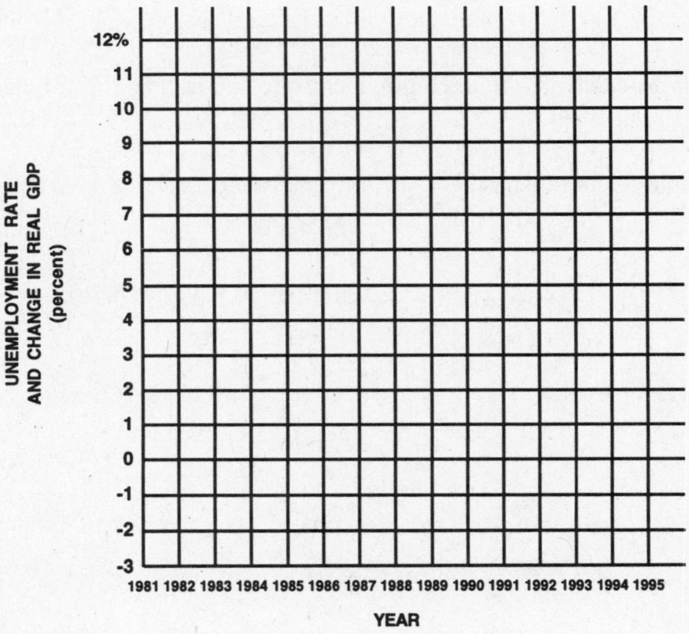

142

3. The relationship between the unemployment rate and the percentage change in the real GDP is best characterized as:
    (a) A direct relationship (the two indicators go up and down together).
    (b) An inverse relationship (the two indicators move in opposite directions).

4. Which indicator seems to change direction first as time passes?
    (a) Percentage change in real GDP.
    (b) The unemployment rate.

5. Which of the following kinds of unemployment is reflected in the fluctuations in Figure 10.1?
    (a) Structural unemployment.
    (b) Seasonal unemployment.
    (c) Cyclical unemployment.
    (d) Frictional unemployment.

6. In what years was full employment, as defined by the text, achieved   between 1981 and 1995?

Exercise 2

This exercise shows the relationship between unemployment and population. It is similar to the problem at the end of the chapter.

Suppose the data in Table 10.2 describe a nation's population.

Table 10.2. Employment and unemployment

	Year 1	Year 2
Population	400 million	460 million
Labor force	250 million	250 million
Unemployment rate	8 percent	8 percent
Number of unemployed	_____	_____
Number of employed	_____	_____

1. Fill in the blanks in Table 10.2 to show the number of unemployed and the number of employed.

2. When the population grows but the labor force and the unemployment rate remain constant, the number employed (rises, remains the same, falls).

3. If both the population and the number employed remain constant, but a larger percentage of the population passes through to retirement, the unemployment rate should (rise, remain the same, fall), *ceteris paribus.*

4. The people who immigrate to the United States are generally young and of working age compared to the existing population of the United States. As greater immigration rates are permitted and if the unemployment rate stays constant, the number employed would (rise, remain the same, fall), *ceteris paribus.*

5. Suppose each employee contributes $30,000 worth of goods and services to the GDP. If the unemployment rate rises from 5 percent to 8 percent, by how much would GDP decline? _____

143

Exercise 3

The following exercise provides practice in categorizing the various kinds of unemployment. Identify each of the following cases as an example of seasonal unemployment, frictional unemployment, structural unemployment, or cyclical unemployment.

1. The immigration service faces its greatest problem during the summer when illegal immigrants cross the border to pick crops. _____

2. People who are fired from jobs with high salaries take longer to find new jobs than those with low salaries. _____

3. At the worst point of the Great Depression nearly one-fourth of the labor force in the United States was unemployed. _____

4. In some cities there are extreme shortages of labor at the same time that there is substantial unemployment. The problem is that the shortages occur in high-tech industries while the unemployment occurs for unskilled workers. _____

Exercise 4

This exercise will help you see the impact of different inflation rates on the value of money held for different periods of time.

1. Use Table 10.3 in the text to find the value of $1000 for the given inflation rate and period of time.
   a. Four years at 8% inflation: _____
   b. Five years at 4% inflation: _____
   c. Eight years at 4% inflation: _____
   d. Ten years at 2% inflation: _____
   e. Seven years at 10% inflation: _____

2. In which of the two cases above does the $1000 come closest to being worth the same amount?

3. In which case above is the $1000 worth the least amount?

4. Would you lose more money if you placed $1000 under your mattress for ten years at 2% inflation or if you placed $1000 in a cookie jar for four years at 8% inflation?

Common Errors

The first statement in each "common error" below is incorrect. Each incorrect statement is followed by a corrected version and an explanation.

1. The government should eliminate unemployment. WRONG!
   The government must lower unemployment at the same time that it accomplishes other goals. RIGHT!
   Under the Full Employment and Balanced Growth Act of 1978, the government sets an unemployment goal for itself, but this goal is well short of a zero unemployment rate. As we shall see in subsequent chapters, the government may have to sacrifice such goals as price stability if it lowers unemployment too much. In this chapter we have seen that it would be very difficult and even undesirable to eliminate frictional or seasonal unemployment.

2.   A rise in the unemployment rate of 0.1 or 0.2 percent for a month is bad. WRONG!
Monthly changes in the unemployment rate may not have any significant economic implications. RIGHT!
        Small changes in the unemployment rate tell us nothing about what is happening to disguised
unemployment (people who seem to be working but are not), discouraged workers (people who are no
longer looking), or changes in the labor force; and large changes in seasonal or frictional unemployment
are not necessarily bad and could not be easily remedied even if they were. Be careful in interpreting
short-run changes in the unemployment rate.

3.   When the price of a product rises, there is inflation. WRONG!
When an average of prices rises, there is inflation. RIGHT!
        The price of a single product may rise while an average of prices of all products falls. Such
adjustment in relative prices is essential to the most *efficient* distribution of goods and services through
the market. When the average of all prices is rising, however, distribution may not be efficient and
redistributions of income may occur.

4.   As long as price increases do not exceed the inflation rate, they do not contribute to inflation. WRONG!
Every price increase contributes to a rise in the inflation rate. RIGHT!
        Since the inflation rate is an average of all price increases, the increase in any price by any amount
raises the average. Firms that buy commodities from other firms that raise prices will in turn pass the
increase on to their own customers; an increased price may have indirect effects in raising the inflation
rate.

■ ANSWERS ■

Using Key Terms

Across
6. deflation
7. unemployment rate
8. relative price
10. real income
12. unemployment
13. business cycle
15. nominal income
16. recession

Down
1. Consumer Price Index
2. full employment
3. price stability
4. inflation
5. inflation rate
9. macroeconomics
11. labor force
14. real GDP

True or False

1. T
2. F The production of goods and services in the U.S. has not been a smooth rising trend but has been
       characterized by periods of economic growth and recessions. See Figure 10.9 in the text.
3. F During the business cycle, unemployment and production typically move in opposite directions.
4. F This person is considered to be frictionally unemployed.
5. T

6. F There will always be some frictional and structural unemployment. By "full employment" we mean the lowest level of unemployment consistent with price stability.
7. T
8. F Some people gain and some people lose during periods of inflation.
9. T
10. T

Multiple Choice

1. a	5. a	9. d	13. d	17. b
2. b	6. b	10. c	14. b	18. c
3. c	7. b	11. a	15. a	19. c
4. a	8. d	12. d	16. d	20. b

Problems and Applications

Exercise 1

1. **Table 10.1 Answer**

Year	(4) Unemployment rate (percent)
1981	7.6
1982	9.7
1983	9.6
1984	7.5
1985	7.2
1986	7.0
1987	6.2
1988	5.5
1989	5.3
1990	5.5
1991	6.7
1992	7.4
1993	6.8
1994	6.1
1995	5.6

2. **Figure 10.1 Answer**

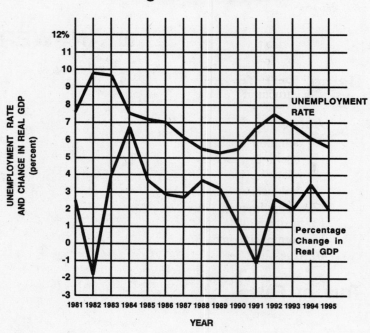

3. b
4. a After a dramatic rise in real GDP, it takes several years for the unemployment rate to reach the lowest level.
5. c
6. 1988, 1989, 1990

146

Exercise 2

1. Table 10.2 answer

	Year 1	Year 2
Population	400 million	460 million
Labor force	250 million	250 million
Unemployment rate	8 percent	8 percent
Number of unemployed	20 million (= 250 x 0.08)	20 million
Number of employed	230 million (= 250 – 20)	230 million

2. Remains the same
3. Fall
4. Rise
5. With 3 percent (8 percent – 5 percent) of the labor force newly unemployed, there are 7.5 million unemployed (= 3 percent x 250 million in the labor force). They could have produced an average of $30,000 a year for a total of $225 billion (= 7.5 million x $30,000) in GDP.

Exercise 3

1. seasonal
2. frictional
3. cyclical
4. structural

Exercise 4

1. a. $735
   b. $822
   c. $731
   d. $820
   e. $513
2. b and d
3. e
4. $1000 in a cookie jar for four years at 8% inflation

147

CHAPTER 11

Aggregate Supply and Demand

Quick Review

- The primary outcomes of the macroeconomy include output (GDP), prices, jobs, growth, and international balances. These outcomes result from the interplay of internal market forces, external shocks, and policy levers. A macro model is necessary to guide policy makers as they devise policies aimed at controlling the business cycle.

- According to the Classical model, the economy "self-adjusts" to deviations from the long-run growth trend and thus should simply be left alone. The cornerstone of the Classical view is flexible wages and prices, which are embedded in Say's Law, which states that "supply creates its own demand." The Great Depression weakened faith in the Classical beliefs.

- Writing during the 1930s, John Maynard Keynes developed an alternative model. He asserted that the private economy was inherently unstable, and because of that inherent instability government intervention was required. This contrasted sharply with the "hands off" Classical view.

- The debate between the Keynesians and the Classical view can be best understood using the tools of aggregate supply and demand. Aggregate demand (AD), the demand for all goods and services, refers to the various quantities of output that all market participants are willing and able to buy at alternative price levels in a given period, *ceteris paribus*. It slopes downward to the right because a decrease in the price level causes an increase in real balances (real balances effect), an increase in net exports (foreign trade effect), and a decrease in the interest rate (interest rate effect).

- Aggregate supply (AS) represents the total quantity of output producers are willing and able to supply at all alternative price levels in a given time period, *ceteris paribus*. It slopes upward to the right because an increase in the price level causes profit margins to widen and factor costs to rise.

- The intersection of aggregate supply and demand determines macro equilibrium. However, macro equilibrium may occur at price and output levels that do not satisfy our macroeconomic goals concerning full employment, growth, and price stability.

- Shifts in AS and AD cause the business cycle. Macro controversies focus on the shape of AS and AD and the potential to shift the two curves. Keynesian theory focuses on AD and the use of government spending or tax changes to shift AD. Monetary theory also focuses on the demand side but stresses the importance of money and credit. Supply-side theory focuses on policies to shift the AS curve such as tax incentives and government deregulation. Eclectic theories draw from both sides of the market.

Learning Objectives

After studying the chapter and doing the following exercises you should:

1. Know the determinants and outcomes of the macroeconomy.
2. Be able to contrast the Classical and Keynesian views of how the economy works.
3. Be able to explain the downward slope of the aggregate demand curve.
4. Be able to explain the upward slope of the aggregate supply curve.
5. Be able to demonstrate macro equilibrium using aggregate supply and demand.
6. Understand inflation and unemployment as macro problems.
7. Be able to distinguish demand-side, supply-side, and eclectic approaches to stabilization.
8. Understand how fiscal, monetary, and supply-side policies shift the aggregate supply and demand curves.
9. Know the history of economic policy during the 1960s, 1970s, 1980s, and 1990s.

Using Key Terms

Fill in the puzzle on the opposite page with the appropriate term from the list of Terms to Remember on page 257 in the text.

Across
1. Depicted on the horizontal axis in Figure 11.3 in the text.
4. The problem illustrated in Figure 11.6 in the text because equilibrium output is less than full employment
5. The use of government spending and taxes to shift the aggregate demand curve.
7. The curve drawn in Figure 11.3 in the text.
10. The upward sloping curve in Figure 11.5 in the text.
11. The macro failure in Figure 11.6 in the text because the equilibrium price level exceeds the desired price level.
12. Occurs as a result of shifts in aggregate demand and aggregate supply.

Down
2. Represented by point E in Figure 11.5 in the text.
3. The use of tax cuts and government deregulation to shift the aggregate supply curve.
6. The idea that whatever is produced by suppliers will always be sold.
8. The area of study that focuses on output, jobs, prices, and growth for the entire economy.
9. The use of money and credit controls to shift the aggregate demand curve.

Puzzle 11.1

True or False: *Circle your choice and explain why any false statements are incorrect.*

T   F   1. Most modern economists believe that the macroeconomy could perform best without government intervention in the form of policy levers.

T   F   2. According to the Classical economists, when consumer demand decreases, workers do not have to lose their jobs because wages and prices will also decrease.

T   F   3. Keynesian economists would advocate a laissez-faire policy during periods of high unemployment and low output.

T   F   4. If, at the prevailing price level, the aggregate quantity supplied exceeds the aggregate quantity demanded, the price level will tend to rise.

T   F   5. The real balances effect says that consumers buy more goods when the price level falls because each dollar has more purchasing power.

T   F   6. One reason why the quantity of real output supplied rises with the price level, *ceteris paribus*, is because profits are higher.

T   F   7. Macro equilibrium never occurs at an output level that provides less than full employment, according to Keynesian economists.

T   F   8. Business cycles are the result of changes in real GDP caused by shifts in aggregate demand and aggregate supply.

T   F   9. Fiscal policy is the use of the government's tax and spending powers to shift the aggregate demand curve.

T   F 10. Monetary policy emphasizes the role of money and interest rates in shifting the aggregate supply curve.

Multiple Choice: *Select the correct answer.*

_____D_____ 1. Which of the following is a determinant of macro outcomes?
    (a) Technological change.
    (b) A major earthquake.
    (c) An increase in the money supply.
    (d) All of the above could be determinants.

_____ 2. Which of the following is a measure of overall economic well-being (i.e., a macro outcome) for the United States?
    (a) The U.S. unemployment rate.
    (b) U.S. population growth.
    (c) A change in the supply of money in the U.S.
    (d) Turmoil in Asian economies.

3. Which of the following characterizes the Classical view of the economy?
   (a) Wages are flexible but prices are not.
   (b) The economy is inherently unstable.
   (c) Flexible prices and wages will allow the economy to self-adjust to full employment.
   (d) Government policies can stabilize the economy.

4. Say's Law implies that:
   (a) Increased prices lead to increased supply.
   (b) Full employment can never exist at macro equilibrium.
   (c) Whatever is produced will be sold.
   (d) Wages and prices are inflexible thus preventing any macro equilibrium.

5. Keynes viewed the economy as inherently unstable and suggested that during an economic downturn policy makers should:
   (a) Cut taxes or increase government spending.
   (b) Cut taxes or reduce government spending.
   (c) Raise taxes or increase government spending.
   (d) Raise taxes or reduce government spending.

6. The upward slope of the aggregate supply curve can best be explained by:
   (a) The real balance effect.
   (b) The interest-rate effect.
   (c) The higher costs associated with higher capacity utilization rates.
   (d) The concept that consumers tend to buy more goods as the price level rises.

7. When the price level in our economy falls relative to the price level in foreign economies, consumers tend to:
   (a) Buy more imported goods and fewer domestically produced goods, *ceteris paribus*.
   (b) Buy more imported goods and more domestic goods, *ceteris paribus*.
   (c) Buy fewer imported goods and more domestic goods, *ceteris paribus*.
   (d) Buy fewer imported goods and fewer domestic goods, *ceteris paribus*.

8. The real balance effect relies on the idea that as the price level falls:
   (a) Each dollar you own will purchase more goods and services.
   (b) Each bond you own will increase in value, thus increasing your wealth.
   (c) You will begin to save less because your wealth has increased.
   (d) All of the above are the case.

9. At the intersection of the aggregate supply and aggregate demand curves, the economy is experiencing:
   (a) Full employment.
   (b) Macro equilibrium.
   (c) Low levels of inflation.
   (d) All of the above.

10. Refer to Figure 11.5 in the text. At a price of P_1:
    (a) A surplus exists equal to $S_1 - Q_E$.
    (b) A surplus exists equal to $S_1 - D_1$.
    (c) A shortage exists equal to $S_1 - Q_E$.
    (d) A shortage exists equal to $S_1 - D_1$.

11. Which of the following causes the aggregate supply curve to shift, *ceteris paribus*?
    (a) An increase in the cost of raw materials.
    (b) Lower business taxes.
    (c) An easing of environmental regulations.
    (d) All of the above could shift aggregate supply.

12. Which of the following causes the aggregate demand curve to increase, *ceteris paribus*?
    (a) The Asian currency crisis of 1997-98.
    (b) Increased interest rates.
    (c) Reduced income taxes.
    (d) A stock market crash.

13. If an economy is at macro equilibrium and aggregate supply decreases:
    (a) The unemployment rate will decrease and the price level will increase.
    (b) Both the unemployment rate and price level will increase.
    (c) The unemployment rate will increase and the price level will decrease.
    (d) Both the unemployment rate and price level will decrease.

14. Controversies between Keynesian, monetarist, supply-side, and eclectic theories focus on:
    (a) The shape and sensitivity of aggregate supply and aggregate demand curves.
    (b) The existence or nonexistence of the aggregate supply curve.
    (c) The importance of international balances to the economy.
    (d) The usefulness of using aggregate demand and supply to analyze adjustment of the macro equilibrium.

15. Refer to the Headline article on external shocks on page 251 in the text. What is likely to happen to U.S. imports from Asian countries as a result of the Asian currency crisis, *ceteris paribus*?
    (a) Increase, due to the relatively stronger dollar.
    (b) Decrease, due to the relatively weaker Asian currencies.
    (c) There will probably be no impact on U.S. imports.
    (d) Increase along with U.S. exports.

16. Which of the following economic perspectives focus on aggregate demand to explain the changes in unemployment and inflation?
    (a) Classical and supply-side.
    (b) Keynesian and monetarist.
    (c) Classical and Keynesian.
    (d) New Classical and Keynesian.

17. A tax cut can best be characterized as:
    (a) Monetary policy only.
    (b) Fiscal policy only.
    (c) Both monetary and supply-side policy.
    (d) Both fiscal and supply-side policy.

18. Individual employment and training programs are policy levers most likely to be advocated by:
    (a) Classical economists.
    (b) Neoclassical economists.
    (c) Keynesians.
    (d) Supply-side economists.

19. Monetary policy involves:
    (a) The use of money and credit controls to influence the macro economy.
    (b) Changes in government spending.
    (c) Changes in taxes.
    (d) Shifting the aggregate supply curve.

20. Which of the following types of government policy levers were *tried but found not* effective during the 1970s in the U.S.? (select two)
    (a) Fiscal policy.
    (b) Monetary policy.
    (c) Supply-side policy.
    (d) Classical policy.

Problems and Applications

Exercise 1

This exercise examines the effects of fiscal policy using aggregate supply and demand curves.

Assume the aggregate demand curve (D_1) and aggregate supply curve (S_1) are those shown in Figure 11.1. Then suppose the government increases spending, which causes the quantity of output demanded in the economy to rise by \$1 trillion per year at every price level. Decide whether the change shifts aggregate demand or aggregate supply from its initial position.

Figure 11.1

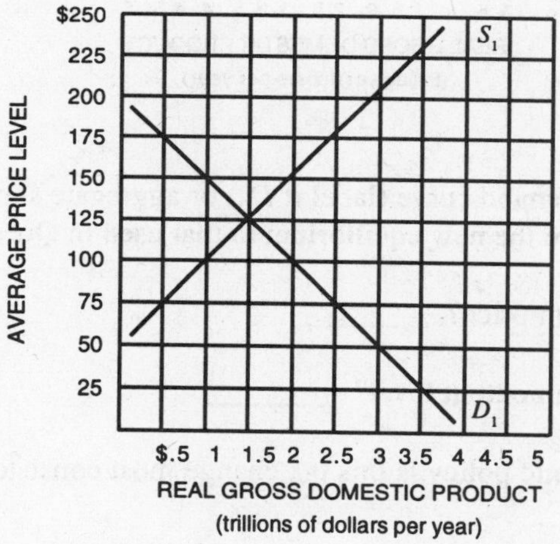

1. Draw the new aggregate demand curve (label it D_2) or aggregate supply curve (label it S_2) in Figure 11.1.

2. What is the new equilibrium average price? _____

3. What is the new equilibrium output level? _____

4. Which school of thought would be most likely to prescribe the use of fiscal policy in this way?
   _____

155

5. The shift that occurred in Question 1 (above) is consistent with:
   (a) Stagflation (inflation and a higher unemployment rate).
   (b) Inflation and a lower unemployment rate.
   (c) Deflation and a higher unemployment rate.
   (d) Lower inflation and a lower unemployment rate.

Exercise 2

Suppose corporate taxes are reduced to encourage productivity and as a result firms (sellers) lower prices by an average of $50 per unit of output. In Questions 1–5, compare the new equilibrium to that established in Figure 11.2. Decide whether the change shifts aggregate demand or aggregate supply from its initial position.

Figure 11.2

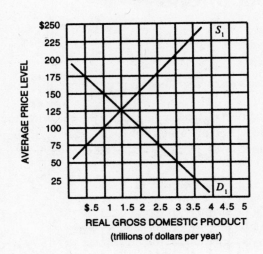

1. Draw the new aggregate demand curve (label it D_2) or aggregate supply curve (label it S_2) in Figure 11.2. Compare the new equilibrium to that used in Questions 1–5 in Exercise 1.

2. What is the new equilibrium price? _____

3. What is the new equilibrium output level? _____

4. With which type of economic policy is this tax change most consistent? _____

5. This shift is consistent with:
   (a) Stagflation (inflation and a higher unemployment rate).
   (b) Inflation and a lower unemployment rate.
   (c) Deflation and a higher unemployment rate.
   (d) A lower price level and lower unemployment rate.

Exercise 3

This exercise will help to show how aggregate demand and supply can be used to analyze the effects of government policy. Suppose the aggregate demand curve and aggregate supply curve for all of the goods in an economy are presented in Figure 11.3. The economy is assumed to be on aggregate demand curve B in the current fiscal year.

156

Figure 11.3

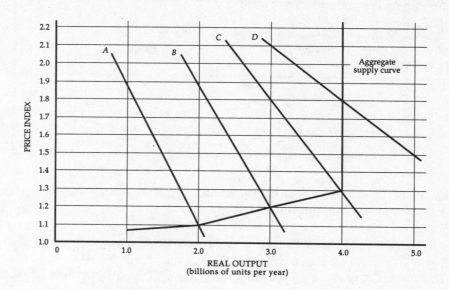

1. Four aggregate demand curves (A, B, C, and D) are shown in Figure 11.3 corresponding to four alternative government policies for the coming fiscal year.

    For the following four government policies, choose the aggregate demand curve in Figure 11.3 that best portrays the expected impact of each policy. Place the letter of your choice in each blank provided.

    a. _C or D_   Money supply is expanded, taxes are cut, government increases its expenditures.

    b. _b_   Government does nothing.

    c. _A_   Government decides to balance the budget by reducing government spending and by raising taxes.

    d. _C or D_   Government increases expenditures and cuts taxes.

2. Indicate the equilibrium price index for each policy in Table 11.1.

    Table 11.1. Equilibrium prices for four government policies

Aggregate demand curve	A	B	C	D
Equilibrium price index	____	____	____	____

3. Suppose the price index is currently 1.2 as shown by demand curve B in Figure 11.3. Compute the inflation rate under each of the four policies assuming the supply curve remains the same. The formula is:

    $$\frac{\text{equilibrium price index} - 1.2}{1.2} \times 100\%$$

    Enter your answers for each policy in the appropriate blank of column 1 in Table 11.2.

157

Table 11.2. Inflation rates, equilibrium output, and unemployment rates under four government policies

Aggregate demand curve	(1) Equilibrium price change	(2) Equilibrium output (billions of units per year)	(3) Unemployment rate
A	_____%	_____	_____%
B	_____	_____	_____
C	_____	_____	_____
D	_____	_____	_____

4. In column 2 of Table 11.2 indicate the equilibrium output associated with each of the policies. Use Figure 11.3 to find this information.

5. Which of the following should be used to calculate the U.S. unemployment rate?
   (a) The U.S. population divided by the U.S. labor force times 100%.
   (b) The number of people employed divided by the U.S. population times 100%.
   (c) The number of people counted as unemployed divided by the U.S. labor force times 100%.
   (d) The number of people unemployed divided by the U.S. population times 100%.

6. Table 11.3 shows a *hypothetical* U.S. population, the labor force, the number of people who are employed, and the number of people who are unemployed at each production rate for the economy. Compute the unemployment rate at each production rate in the table.

Table 11.3. Computation of the unemployment rate

Production rate (billions of units per year)	2	3	4
U.S. population (millions)	200	200	200
Labor force (millions)	100	100	100
Number of people unemployed (millions)	15	8	5
Number of people employed (millions)	85	92	95
Unemployment rate (percent)	_____	_____	_____

7. Using the information in Table 11.3, complete column 3 in Table 11.2, which shows the unemployment rate corresponding to each government policy.

8. The government's dilemma is:
   (a) That it cannot reach an unemployment level of 5 percent without experiencing inflation of at least 8 percent.
   (b) That it cannot reach stable prices (0 percent increase) without experiencing an unemployment rate of 8 percent or more.
   (c) That when it makes gains in holding inflation below 8 percent, unemployment increases.
   (d) Expressed by all of the above statements.

9. Which of the four aggregate demand curves places the economy closest to full-employment output and moderate inflation?
   (a) Aggregate demand curve *A*.
   (b) Aggregate demand curve *B*.
   (c) Aggregate demand curve *C*.
   (d) Aggregate demand curve *D*.

Exercise 4

Reread the Headline article in the text entitled "A Tax Cut for Capital Gains." Then answer the following questions.

1. What is the expected impact on aggregate demand if the capital gains tax is cut?

2. Cite some evidence to support this perspective.

Common Errors

The first statement in each "common error" below is incorrect. Each incorrect statement is followed by a corrected version and an explanation.

1. Full employment is achieved at the equilibrium GDP. WRONG!
   Full employment is not necessarily achieved at the equilibrium GDP. RIGHT!
   When resources are fully employed, no additional goods and services can be produced. However, equilibrium GDP refers to the equality between the aggregate demand for goods and services and the aggregate supply of goods and services, not to any particular level of resource employment.

2. Aggregate demand (supply) and market demand (supply) are the same. WRONG!
   Aggregate demand (supply) and market demand (supply) involve very different levels of aggregation. RIGHT!
   Market demand can be found for specific markets only. Products in each market must be homogeneous. The firms in that market are competitors. The market demand is used for microeconomic applications. Aggregate demand applies to all markets within the economy and involves their average prices. It is not even possible to sum the market demand curves to find the aggregate demand curve because the prices of different commodities cannot be measured in the same units; an average price must be computed. Aggregate demand is used for macroeconomic applications, not microeconomic ones. The distinction between aggregate supply and market supply is similar to that between aggregate demand and market demand.

■ ANSWERS ■

Using Key Terms

Across

1. real GDP
4. unemployment
5. fiscal policy
7. aggregate demand
10. aggregate supply
11. inflation
12. business cycle

Down

2. equilibrium (macro)
3. supply-side policy
6. Say's Law
8. macroeconomics
9. monetary policy

True or False

1. F   Most modern economists believe that some government intervention is necessary for the macro economy to perform properly.
2. T
3. F   Keynesian economists would advocate government policies to increase the level of spending in the economy.
4. F   The price level will tend to fall because a surplus of goods and services exists.
5. T
6. T
7. F   Macro equilibrium does not guarantee full employment; it only guarantees that aggregate demand equals aggregate supply.
8. T
9. T
10. F   Monetary policy attempts to shift the aggregate demand curve.

Multiple Choice

1. d	5. a	9. b	13. b	17. d
2. a	6. c	10. b	14. a	18. d
3. c	7. c	11. d	15. a	19. a
4. c	8. d	12. c	16. b	20. a, b

Problems and Applications

Exercise 1

1. See Figure 11.1 answer, D_2.

Figure 11.1 Answer

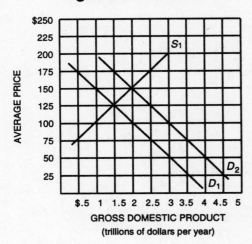

2. $150
3. $2 trillion
4. Keynesian
5. b

Exercise 2

1. See Figure 11.2 answer, S_2.

Figure 11.2 Answer

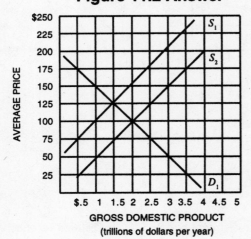

2. $100
3. $2 trillion
4. Supply-side policy
5. d

Exercise 3

1. a. *C* or *D*
   b. *B*
   c. *A*
   d. *C* or *D*

2. **Table 11.1 Answer**

Aggregate demand curve	A	B	C	D
Equilibrium price index	1.1	1.2	1.3	1.8

3. See Table 11.2 answer, column 1.

Table 11.2 Answer

Aggregate demand curve	(1) Equilibrium price change	(2) Equilibrium output (billions of units per year)	(3) Unemployment rate
A	− 8.3%	2.0	15%
B	0.0	3.0	8
C	8.3	4.0	5
D	50.0	4.0	5

4. See Table 11.2 answer, column 2.
5. c

6. **Table 11.3 Answer**

Production rate (billions of units per year)	2	3	4
Unemployment rate (percent)	15	8	5

7. See Table 11.2 answer, column 3.
8. d
9. c

Exercise 4

1. Proponents expect aggregate demand to increase.

2. The article states that "Past capital gains cuts have led to investment booms ... " Investment is one of the components of aggregate demand.

CHAPTER 12

Fiscal Policy

Quick Review

- The four components of aggregate demand are consumption, investment, government spending, and net exports (exports minus imports).

- Consumption spending refers to all household spending on goods and services. Investment refers to spending by business on new plant and equipment and net changes in inventory. Government spending includes expenditure on goods and services at the state, federal, and local level. It does not include spending that results in income transfers such as social security payments, which are payments for which no goods or services are exchanged. Net exports is the difference between spending on exports and spending on imports.

- The four components of aggregate demand represent a schedule of planned purchases that will change as the price level changes, as illustrated by the aggregate demand curve. Equilibrium (macro) will occur where aggregate demand and aggregate supply intersect, but this may not be at the level which achieves our price level, income, and employment goals.

- If the level of aggregate demand results in an equilibrium that is different than the full-employment output level, there is a GDP gap. Fiscal policy can be used to change the level of aggregate demand.

- If aggregate demand is deficient, the government can provide fiscal stimulus by increasing its spending or by cutting taxes. Increased government spending generates additional consumption in the economy, which is referred to as the multiplier effect. The multiplier determines the change in total spending because of an initial change in spending. The marginal propensity to consume (MPC) is the fraction of additional income that is spent. The multiplier is equal to 1/1 – MPC. If taxes are cut, disposable income increases and so does consumption. Investment spending can be encouraged by tax cuts as well. In both cases there is a multiplier effect.

- If aggregate demand is too great and the problem is inflationary pressure, the government can provide fiscal restraint by decreasing its spending or increasing taxes. The multiplier will then work in reverse.

- The primary fiscal policy lever used to manage aggregate demand is the federal government's budget. As a result, there is typically a budget deficit or surplus. A balanced budget is appropriate only if the resulting aggregate demand is consistent with full-employment equilibrium.

Learning Objectives

After reading the chapter and doing the following exercises you should:

1. Know the four components of aggregate demand and what is included in each of them.
2. Understand the multiplier process.
3. Understand the role of the MPC and the MPS in the multiplier process.
4. Be able to calculate the spending multiplier.
5. Be able to describe fiscal policies to increase aggregate demand.
6. Be able to describe fiscal policies to reduce aggregate demand.
7. Understand the arguments in favor of, and against, balancing the federal budget.

Using Key Terms

Fill in the puzzle on the opposite page with the appropriate term from the list of Terms to Remember on page 278 in the text.

Across
4. Equal to 0.25 in Figure 12.5 in the text.
6. A schedule of planned expenditures as illustrated in Figure 12.2 in the text.
10. Equal to −1% of aggregate demand in Figure 12.1 in the text.
11. The part of disposable income that is not spent.
12. Occurs at point b in Figure 12.4 in the text.
13. An example is a decrease in government spending to reduce inflation.
14. Equal to 69% of aggregate demand in Figure 12.1 in the text.

Down
1. The fraction of additional income spent by consumers.
2. According to the article in the text, the objective of Clinton's tax credit for families with children is to increase _____.
3. Tends to increase when corporate taxes are cut.
5. Equal to approximately $290 billion for 1992 in Figure 12.9 in the text.
7. The difference in Q_1 and Q_F in Figure 12.4 in the text.
8. The excess of government revenues over government expenditures.
9. Equal to 4 in Table 12.1 in the text.

Puzzle 12.1

True or False: *Circle your choice and explain why any false statements are incorrect.*

T   F   1. During the Great Depression, the primary reason why unemployment was so high was because unemployed workers were unskilled.

T   F   2. The four components of aggregate demand are consumption, investment, government expenditures, and net exports.

T   F   3. To an economist, the term "investment" refers to the purchase of stocks, for example.

T   F   4. Social security payments are not included in aggregate demand because they do not reflect a purchase of goods and services.

T   F   5. Aggregate demand is a single value unrelated to the price level.

T   F   6. Equilibrium GDP is always the most desired level of GDP for an economy.

T   F   7. The GDP gap represents the value of goods and services that could have been produced by the economy but were not due to inadequate aggregate demand.

T   F   8. The total impact on aggregate demand of increased government expenditures includes both the new government expenditures plus all subsequent increases in consumption caused by the additional government outlays.

T   F   9. The best government policy during a recession, *ceteris paribus*, is to balance the federal budget.

T   F   10. The greater the upward slope of the aggregate supply curve, the greater the increase in the price level when aggregate demand increases.

Multiple Choice: *Select the correct answer.*

    1. In developing his theory of unemployment during the Great Depression, Keynes:
   (a) Focused primarily on improving the skills of the unemployed.
   (b) Focused on the stimulation of the economy by shifting aggregate supply.
   (c) Explained how aggregate demand could be inadequate to ensure full employment.
   (d) Dealt only with the causes of unemployment and not policies to correct the problem.

    2. Which type of expenditure is typically the largest component of aggregate demand?
   (a) Consumption.
   (b) Government expenditures.
   (c) Business investment.
   (d) Net exports.

_D_ 3. At the intersection of aggregate supply and aggregate demand, the economy experiences:
(a) Full employment.
(b) High levels of unemployment.
(c) Inflation.
(d) Any of the above could occur.

_C_ 4. When aggregate demand exceeds the full-employment level of output, the result is:
(a) Significant unemployment.
(b) Higher inventory levels.
(c) A higher average price level.
(d) A recession.

_B_ 5. Keynes argued that the level of economic activity is primarily related to:
(a) Aggregate supply.
(b) Aggregate demand.
(c) The money supply.
(d) Interest rates.

_D_ 6. If an economy has a GDP gap, such that equilibrium output is less than full-employment output, which of the following fiscal policies will reduce the gap?
(a) A tax increase.
(b) An increase in the money supply.
(c) A reduction in Social Security payments.
(d) An increase in government expenditures on highways and bridges.

_D_ 7. The multiplier effect exists because of:
(a) The circular nature of the economy.
(b) The fact that money is spent and respent multiple times.
(c) One person's spending becomes another person's income.
(d) All of the above.

_B_ 8. Which of the following would be a Keynesian solution for inflation?
(a) Increase transfer payments to those people hurt by inflation.
(b) Decrease government expenditures and let the multiplier work.
(c) Restrict foreign imports into the country.
(d) Do nothing because the economy is inherently stable.

_D_ 9. If, in the aggregate, consumers spend 80 cents out of every extra dollar received:
(a) The MPS is 0.20.
(b) The MPC is 0.80.
(c) The multiplier is 5.
(d) All of the above.

_A_ 10. If disposable income in an economy is $300 billion, consumption is $200 billion and the MPC is 0.9, what would the new level of consumption be if disposable income increased to $350 billion, *ceteris paribus*?
(a) $245 billion.
(b) $45 billion.
(c) $250 billion.
(d) $315 billion.

_C_ 11. Refer to Figure 12.7 in the text. The change in spending in the second cycle caused the aggregate demand curve to shift to the right by:
(a) $100 billion.
(b) $400 billion.
(c) $75 billion.
(d) $175 billion.

_A_ 12. Which of the following economies has the highest multiplier?
(a) Economy A with an MPS of 0.1.
(b) Economy B with an MPS of 0.25.
(c) Economy C with an MPC of 0.8.
(d) Economy D with an MPC of 0.6.

_B_ 13. Which of the following provides fiscal stimulus to the economy?
(a) Higher interest rates.
(b) Increased government spending on goods and services.
(c) Increased imports.
(d) Reducing inefficient employment of resources.

_D_ 14. The amount of additional aggregate demand generated by increased government spending depends on:
(a) The marginal propensity to consume.
(b) The number of spending cycles that occur in a given period of time.
(c) The size of the initial increase in government spending.
(d) All of the above.

_B_ 15. During an inflationary period it is appropriate for the government to pursue policies that:
(a) Stimulate aggregate demand.
(b) Reduce aggregate demand.
(c) Make budget deficits larger.
(d) Eliminate the public debt.

_D_ 16. Which of the following will definitely reduce a budget deficit and provide fiscal restraint?
(a) Greater government spending and lower taxes.
(b) Greater government spending and higher taxes.
(c) Lower government spending and lower taxes.
(d) Lower government spending and higher taxes.

_C_ 17. When we compare the total impact on aggregate demand of a $50 billion increase in government expenditures and a $50 billion decrease in taxes we find that:
(a) The total impact on aggregate demand of the two policies will be the same.
(b) The total impact on aggregate demand will be the same but in opposite directions.
(c) The increase in government expenditures will have a greater total impact on aggregate demand.
(d) The decrease in taxes will have a greater total impact on aggregate demand.

_C_ 18. Refer to the Headline article on "Fiscal Stimulus" in the text. Assuming the total reduction in taxes is $36 billion, and the United State's MPC is 0.9, what would the total impact on aggregate demand be as a result of President Clinton's plan, *ceteris paribus*?
(a) An increase of $36 billion.
(b) A decrease of $32.4 billion.
(c) An increase of $324 billion.
(d) A decrease of $360 billion.

168

19. Fiscal policy is most effective in changing the level of real output without causing inflation when the aggregate supply curve is:
   (a) Horizontal.
   (b) Vertical.
   (c) Upward sloping.
   (d) Fiscal policy has no effect on inflation, regardless of the slope of the aggregate supply curve.

A 20. During a recession the appropriate fiscal policy would be for the federal government to:
   (a) Run a budget deficit.
   (b) Run a budget surplus.
   (c) It is always appropriate fiscal policy to balance the budget.
   (d) Match all spending increases with a tax increase.

Problems and Applications

Exercise 1

The following exercise shows how the multiplier works and how to calculate it.

1. Suppose the economy were at full employment but suddenly experienced a $200 billion drop in business expenditures due to abrupt cancellation of investment plans. Follow the impact of this sudden change through the economy by completing Table 12.1. (Refer to Table 12.1 in the text.) Assume the marginal propensity to consume is 0.90. (*Hint*: Consumption will drop by the "amount of the change in spending in the previous cycle" times the MPC.)

Table 12.1

Spending cycles	Drop in investment expenditure	Change in spending (billions of dollars per year)	Cumulative decrease in aggregate spending (billions of dollars per year)
First cycle:	GDP gap emerges	$200	$200
Second cycle:	consumption drops by	_____	_____
Third cycle:	consumption drops by	_____	_____
Fourth cycle:	consumption drops by	_____	_____
Fifth cycle:	consumption drops by	_____	_____
Sixth cycle:	consumption drops by	_____	_____
Seventh cycle:	consumption drops by	_____	_____

2. Compute the multiplier. _____

3. Multiply $200 billion by the multiplier. _____

169

Exercise 2

Reread the Headline article in the text entitled "Consumers' Confidence Up Sharply" from *USA Today*. Then answer the following questions using Figure 12.1 for Question 1.

Figure 12.1

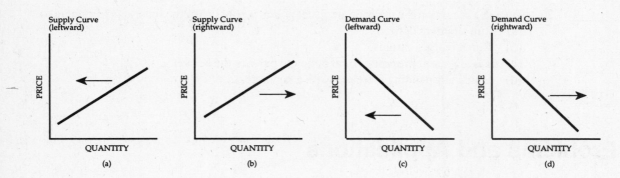

1. Which of the diagrams in Figure 12.1 best represents the shift that can be expected as a result of increased consumer confidence?

    a   b   c   d   (circle one)

2. What other signs, in addition to the consumer confidence index, indicate that the economy is moving forward?

3. Why do economists focus so strongly on consumer confidence as being critical to the health of the economy? Cite some evidence from the article.

Exercise 3

This exercise shows how the multiplier works to eliminate a GDP gap.

Refer to Figure 12.2 to answer the following questions. Assume the MPC equals 0.80 and the current level of aggregate demand is equal to AD_1.

Figure 12.2

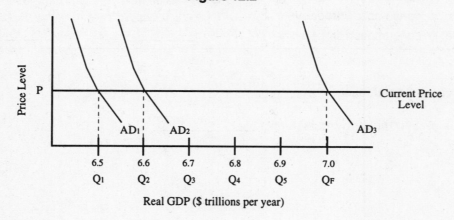

170

1. What is the size of the GDP gap? _____

2. What is the value of the multiplier? _____

3. An increase in government spending of $100 billion would cause consumption to increase by $_____ billion in the second spending cycle.

4. An increase in government spending of $100 billion would cause a cumulative increase in aggregate demand equal to $_____ billion and would result in an equilibrium real GDP equal to $_____ trillion.

Common Errors

The first statement in each "common error" below is incorrect. Each incorrect statement is followed by a corrected version and an explanation.

1. Government deficits always lead to inflation. WRONG!
    Government deficits may result from government spending to reach full employment with price stability. RIGHT!
    You should focus on what is happening to aggregate demand, not just deficits, when looking for the sources of inflation. By looking at the deficit, you cannot tell if the economy is at full employment or not. If there is a recession, government spending and resulting deficits may restore full employment with price stability! If the economy is already at full employment, inflation can result from increased consumption, investment, or export expenditures, just as much as from increased government spending. It is easy to point the finger at the government and forget the contribution to inflation of all of the sectors of the economy.

2. When a person invests in stocks, investment expenditure is increased. WRONG!
    Purchase of stocks has only an indirect relationship to investment expenditure in the economy. RIGHT!
    Investment expenditure refers to purchases of new capital goods (plant, machinery, etc.) or inventories. A purchase of stock represents a transfer of ownership from one person to another. Sometimes such purchases are called "financial investments," but they do not represent economic investment.

3. Aggregate demand rises when people buy more imports. WRONG!
    Aggregate demand falls when people buy more imports, *ceteris paribus*. RIGHT!
    Students often think of imports as expenditures and therefore believe that increased spending on imports will have the same effects on the economy as an increase in consumption. Expenditures on imports, however, do not generate domestic income. If imports increase, they do so at the expense of purchases of U.S. goods, meaning fewer jobs in the United States. Because employment declines, there is less income with which to consume goods; consumption falls and so does aggregate demand.

4. Macro equilibrium and full employment are always the same. WRONG!
    Macro equilibrium and full employment are determined in different ways. RIGHT!
    Macro equilibrium occurs where aggregate demand and aggregate supply intersect. Full employment refers to the use of all available resources in production. If macro equilibrium does not occur at full employment there is a GDP gap.

■ ANSWERS ■

Using Key Terms

Across

4. marginal propensity to save
6. aggregate demand
10. net exports
11. saving
12. equilibrium (macro)
13. fiscal policy
14. consumption

Down

1. marginal propensity to consume
2. disposable income
3. investment
5. budget deficit
7. GDP gap
8. budget surplus
9. multiplier

True or False

1. F   The primary reason was insufficient aggregate demand.
2. T
3. F   Investment, to an economist, represents business expenditures on new plant and equipment plus changes in inventories during a given time period.
4. T
5. F   Aggregate demand is a schedule showing the quantity of output demanded at various price levels.
6. F   Equilibrium GDP is simply the output where aggregate demand and aggregate supply intersect. This may or may not be a desirable output level.
7. T
8. T
9. F   In order to balance the federal budget during a recession, taxes would have to be increased and/or government spending would have to be decreased. Both of these actions are likely to worsen the recession.
10. T

Multiple Choice

1. c	5. b	9. d	13. b	17. c
2. a	6. d	10. a	14. d	18. c
3. d	7. d	11. c	15. b	19. a
4. c	8. b	12. a	16. d	20. a

Problems and Applications

Exercise 1

1. **Table 12.1 Answer**

Spending cycles	Amount	Cumulative decrease in aggregate spending
First cycle:	$200.0	$200.0
Second cycle:	180.0	380.0
Third cycle:	162.0	542.0
Fourth cycle:	145.8	687.8
Fifth cycle:	131.2	819.0
Sixth cycle:	118.1	937.1
Seventh cycle:	106.3	1043.4

2. Multiplier = $1/(1 - MPC) = 1/(1 - 0.9) = 10$
3. 10 x $200 billion per year = $2 trillion per year

Exercise 2

1. d
2. Increased retail spending and increased sales of existing homes.
3. Consumer spending "accounts for about two-thirds of all economic activity."

Exercise 3

1. $7 trillion - $6.5 trillion = $500 billion
2. Multiplier = $1/(1 - MPC) = 1/(1 - 0.8) = 5$
3. $80 billion
4. 5 x $100 billion = $500 billion, $7.0 trillion

CHAPTER 13

Money and Banks

Quick Review

- Money facilitates market exchanges and allows for specialization. It makes an economy more efficient than one that relys on barter. Anything that serves simultaneously as a medium of exchange, a store of value, and a standard of value can be thought of as money.

- The money supply (M1) is composed of transactions accounts, cash balances, and traveler's checks.

- The banking system can create money by making loans. When a bank decides to make a loan, it simply creates a deposit in the transactions account of the borrower. This deposit becomes part of M1.

- In the U.S., the Federal Reserve System requires banks to maintain some minimum ratio of bank reserves to total deposits. Any reserves above the required level are excess reserves. A bank may use its excess reserves to make new loans.

- As the new loans are spent, the dollars flow back into the banking system and additional loans are made. The banking system as a whole can increase the volume of deposits by the amount of the excess reserves times the money multiplier. This process is known as deposit creation.

- Banks perform a strategic role in the economy by transferring money from savers to spenders and by creating additional money by making loans. An increase in the money supply due to borrowing leads to an increase in aggregate demand. A reduction in the money supply leads to a decrease in aggregate demand.

- Deposit creation is constrained by the willingness of market participants to accept checks and to borrow, the willingness of banks to make loans, and the regulations of the Federal Reserve System.

Learning Objectives

After studying the chapter and doing the following exercises you should:

1. Understand the functions performed by money.
2. Know what is included in M1.
3. Know how banks create money by making loans.
4. Understand the function of the required reserve ratio.
5. Be able to calculate the money multiplier.
6. Understand the connection between the banking system and the circular flow of economic activity.
7. Know the constraints on deposit creation.

Using Key Terms

Fill in the puzzle on the opposite page with the appropriate term from the list of Terms to Remember on page 296 in the text.

Across

2. Total reserves minus required reserves.
3. Assets held by a bank to fulfill its deposit obligations.
4. An account that allows direct payment to a third party.
5. Represent a leakage from the flow of money because they cannot be used to make loans.
6. Tends to increase with an increase in the money supply because new loans are used to purchase additional goods and services.
9. The reciprocal of the required reserve ratio.

Down

1. The process by which bank lending causes the money supply to increase.
3. The system of exchange in Russia described in the article on page 283 in the text.
7. Equal to 0.75 in Figure 13.2 in the text.
8. Equal to $1,150 billion according to Figure 13.1 in the text.
9. Throughout history gold coins, tobacco, and bullets have functioned in this role.

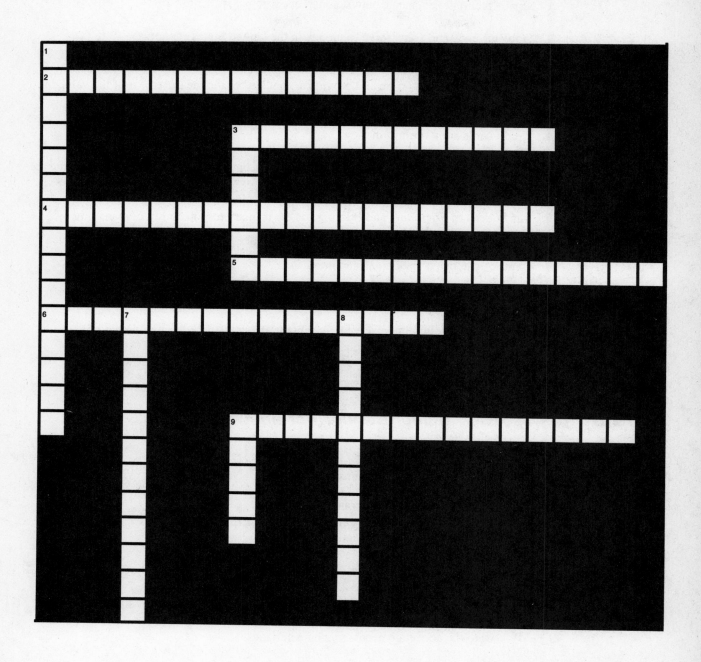

True or False: *Circle your choice and explain why any false statements are incorrect.*

T   F   1. Money facilitates exchange between market participants.

T   F   2. Only currency and coins serve as money in the United States economy.

T   F   3. To be money, an item must be accepted in exchange for goods and services, maintain its value over a period of time and provide a standard for the measurement of the value of goods and services.

T   F   4. Credit cards are a form of money.

T   F   5. Changes in the supply of money affect price level, employment, and output by shifting the aggregate supply curve.

T   F   6. The Bureau of Engraving and Printing has the primary responsibility of managing the money supply in the United States.

T   F   7. In making a loan a bank creates money.

T   F   8. When you deposit a $50 bill in your checking account, M1 increases.

T   F   9. The higher the minimum reserve requirement, the greater the lending power of banks.

T   F   10. A primary function of banks is to transfer money from savers to borrowers.

Multiple Choice: *Select the correct answer.*

 1. Barter:
   (a) Facilitates specialization in production.
   (b) Is most efficient for an economy.
   (c) Is the direct exchange of one good or service for another.
   (d) All of the above are correct.

 2. Which of the following is a necessary characteristic of money?
   (a) It serves as a medium of exchange.
   (b) Its value must be supported by government reserves of gold and silver.
   (c) The government declares it to have value.
   (d) All of the above are necessary characteristics.

 3. The majority of the money supply (M1) in the United States is in the form of:
   (a) Traveler's checks.
   (b) Cash.
   (c) Transactions accounts.
   (d) Gold.

_B_   4. If Bradley takes $100 out of his saving account and hides it under his bed in the form of cash, M1 has:
- (a) Decreased by $100.
- (b) Increased by $100.
- (c) Not changed.
- (d) Increased by more than $100.

_C_   5. Money creation occurs when:
- (a) A person puts cash in a bank.
- (b) A person deposits a payroll check in their checking account.
- (c) Banks make loans to borrowers.
- (d) The Federal Reserve System increases the reserve requirement.

_A_   6. The main goal of banks is to:
- (a) Earn a profit.
- (b) Create money.
- (c) Lend all of their deposits.
- (d) Minimize their reserve ratio.

_C_   7. Which of the following sets the legal minimum-reserve ratio?
- (a) The commercial banks.
- (b) The U.S. Treasury.
- (c) The Federal Reserve System.
- (d) Congress.

_A_   8. Which of the following is the correct way to calculate excess reserves?
- (a) Total reserves minus required reserves.
- (b) The minimum-reserve requirement times transactions account liabilities.
- (c) Total reserves minus the legal minimum-reserve ratio.
- (d) Total reserves plus required reserves.

_D_   9. A bank may lend an amount equal to its:
- (a) Required reserves.
- (b) Total reserves.
- (c) Total assets.
- (d) Excess reserves.

_D_   10. Suppose the total amount of transactions account balances on the books of all of the banks in the system is $1 million and that the minimum reserve ratio is 0.10. The amount of required reserves for the banking system is then:
- (a) $10,000,000.
- (b) $1,000,000.
- (c) $900,000.
- (d) $100,000.

_B_   11. The term "fractional reserves" refers to:
- (a) The fact that reserves are split among many banks.
- (b) Reserves being a small fraction of total transactions accounts.
- (c) The ratio of required reserves to total loans.
- (d) The ratio of excess reserves to total loans.

___C___ 12. If the minimum reserve ratio is 15 percent, the money multiplier is:
  (a) 25.00
  (b) 15.00
  (c) 6.67
  (d) 1.50

___D___ 13. Banks are required to keep a minimum amount of funds in reserve because:
  (a) Depositors may decide to withdrawal funds.
  (b) It provides a constraint on the bank's ability to create money.
  (c) It provides a constraint on the bank's ability to affect aggregate demand.
  (d) All of the above are correct.

___B___ 14. If there were no minimum reserve requirement in the banking system, the potential ability of banks to create money would be:
  (a) Zero.
  (b) Unlimited.
  (c) Limited by the amount of deposits.
  (d) Limited by the number of banks in the banking system.

___A___ 15. Suppose a bank has 2 million dollars in deposits, a required reserve ratio of 20%, and reserves of $500,000. Then it has excess reserves of:
  (a) $100,000.
  (b) $200,000.
  (c) $300,000.
  (d) $500,000.

___B___ 16. Suppose that Maggie finds $10,000 under a bed and deposits her find in her checking account. If the required reserve ratio is 25%, this deposit has the potential of increasing the money supply by:
  (a) $30,000.
  (b) $40,000.
  (c) $2,500.
  (d) $10,000.

___C___ 17. Suppose the entire banking system has a required reserve ratio of 10%. How much could the money supply increase in response to a $1 billion increase in (excess) reserves for the whole banking system?
  (a) $100 million.
  (b) $1 billion.
  (c) $10 billion.
  (d) $9 billion.

___D___ 18. Which of the following is a constraint on deposit creation?
  (a) The willingness of consumers and firms to accept checks in payment for goods and services.
  (b) The willingness of consumers, businesses, and governments to borrow.
  (c) The willingness of banks to loan money to qualified borrowers.
  (d) All of the above.

_B_   19. Banks perform the essential function of:
  - (a) Transferring funds from spenders to savers.
  - (b) Transferring funds from savers to spenders.
  - (c) Keeping the money supply constant.
  - (d) Lending funds to the Federal Reserve Banks.

_D_   20. An increase in the amount of bank loans should shift:
  - (a) The aggregate supply curve to the left.
  - (b) The aggregate supply curve to the right.
  - (c) The aggregate demand curve to the left.
  - (d) The aggregate demand curve to the right.

Problems and Applications

Exercise 1

Use the information from the balance sheet in Table 13.1 to answer Questions 1–5.

Table 13.1. Bank of Arlington

Assets		Liabilities	
Required reserves	$250,000	Transaction accounts	$1,000,000
Other assets	750,000		
Total	$1,000,000	Total	$1,000,000

1. Suppose that the Bank of Arlington is just meeting its reserve requirement. The reserve ratio must be _____, and the money multiplier must be _____.

2. To be in a position to make loans, the Bank of Arlington must acquire some _____ (required reserves, excess reserves).

3. If we assume that the reserve ratio is changed to 15 percent, the Bank of Arlington would have required reserves of _____ and excess reserves of _____.

4. With a 15 percent reserve ratio the Bank of Arlington is in a position to make new loans totaling _____.

5. With a 15 percent reserve ratio, the entire banking system can increase the volume of loans by _____.

Exercise 2

This exercise shows how the multiplier process works.

Assume that all banks in the system lend all of their excess reserves, that the reserve ratio for all banks is 0.20, and that all loans are returned to the banking system in the form of transactions deposits. Use the information from the balance sheets in Table 13.2, Table 13.3, Table 13.4, and Table 13.5 to answer Questions 1–6.

Table 13.2. Bank A - Initial balance sheet

Assets		Liabilities	
Required reserves	$20,000	Transaction accounts	$100,000
Excess reserves	0		
Other assets	80,000		
Total	$100,000	Total	$100,000

1. Bill takes $10,000 out of his cookie jar and deposits it in a transactions account in Bank A. Fill in the blanks in Bank A's balance sheet in Table 13.3 after the deposit. (Remember that some of the deposit will show up in required reserves and the remainder will become part of excess reserves.)

Table 13.3. Bank A - Balance sheet after Bill's deposit

Assets		Liabilities	
Required reserves	$_____	Transaction accounts	$_____
Excess reserves	_____		
Other assets	80,000		
Total	$_____	Total	$_____

Now assume that Bank A lends all of its excess reserves to Pat, who spends the money on a car. The car dealership deposits the money in its transactions account in Bank B. Bank B's initial balance sheet is the same as Bank A's initial balance sheet.

2. Fill in the blanks in Bank B's balance sheet after the car dealership makes its deposit.

Table 13.4. Bank B - Balance sheet after car dealership's deposit

Assets		Liabilities	
Required reserves	$_____	Transaction accounts	$_____
Excess reserves	_____		
Other assets	80,000		
Total	$_____	Total	$_____

Now assume Bank B lends all of its excess reserves to Mary, who spends the money on college tuition. The university deposits the money in Bank C. Bank C's initial balance sheet is the same as Bank A's initial balance sheet.

3. Fill in the blanks in Bank C's balance sheet after the university makes its deposit.

Table 13.5. Bank C - Balance sheet after university's deposit

Assets		Liabilities	
Required reserves	$_____	Transaction accounts	$_____
Excess reserves	_____		
Other assets	80,000		
Total	$_____	Total	$_____

4. Add together the potential increase in loans for each bank because of the initial $10,000 deposit made by Bill.

    Bank A is able to lend $_____
    Bank B is able to lend $_____
    Bank C is able to lend $_____

    Total loans made possible so far $_____

5. The money multiplier for this exercise equals _____.

6. The potential deposit creation for the entire banking system in this exercise is _____.

Common Errors

The first statement in each "common error" below is incorrect. Each incorrect statement is followed by a corrected version and an explanation.

1. Banks can't create money. WRONG!
   Banks can and do create money. RIGHT!
       It should be obvious by now that banks and other depository institutions are very important participants in the money-supply process. They create money by granting loans to borrowers and accomplish their role by adding to their customers' transactions accounts. The accounts are money just as much as the printed money in your wallet is money. The banks create (supply) money, but only in response to borrowers' demands for it. Without customers "demanding" loans, banks wouldn't be able to create money at all.

2. Banks hold your deposits in their vaults. WRONG!
   Banks don't hold your deposits in their vaults. (And neither do other depository institutions.) RIGHT!
       Banks (and other depository institutions) are required by law to hold a fraction of the deposits they receive as reserves. The remaining portion of any deposit may be used by the bank to generate a profit, such as making a loan. Banks will hold a portion of their required reserves in their vault, but some of the required reserves are kept in an account at the Federal Reserve bank.

■ ANSWERS ■

Using Key Terms

Across

2. excess reserves
3. bank reserves
4. transactions accounts
5. required reserves
6. aggregate demand
9. money multiplier

Down

1. deposit creation
3. barter
7. reserve ratio
8. money supply
9. money

True or False

1. T
2. F   Cash is only a small portion of our money supply; most of M1 is in the form of transactions accounts.
3. T
4. F   Credit cards are a payment service. Credit card balances must be paid by cash or check.
5. F   Changes in the supply of money affect the economy by shifting the aggregate demand curve.
6. F   The Federal Reserve System has the primary responsibility of managing the money supply by changing transactions-account balances, not by printing money.
7. T
8. F   The composition of M1 changes (i.e., $50 less cash, $50 more in transactions accounts), but the quantity of M1 does not change.
9. F   The higher the minimum reserve ratio, the lower the excess reserves and the lower the lending power of banks.
10. T

Multiple Choice

1. c	5. c	9. d	13. d	17. c
2. a	6. a	10. d	14. b	18. d
3. c	7. c	11. b	15. a	19. b
4. b	8. a	12. c	16. b	20. d

Problems and Applications

Exercise 1

1. 0.25; 4
2. excess reserves
3. $150,000; $100,000
4. $100,000
5. $666,666.67

184

Exercise 2

1. **Table 13.3 Answer**

Assets		Liabilities	
Required reserves	$22,000	Transaction accounts	$110,000
Excess reserves	8,000		
Other assets	80,000		
Total	$110,000	Total	$110,000

2. **Table 13.4 Answer**

Assets		Liabilities	
Required reserves	$21,600	Transaction accounts	$108,000
Excess reserves	6,400		
Other assets	80,000		
Total	$108,000	Total	$108,000

3. **Table 13.5 Answer**

Assets		Liabilities	
Required reserves	$21,280	Transaction accounts	$106,400
Excess reserves	5,120		
Other assets	80,000		
Total	$106,400	Total	$106,400

4. Bank A lent $8,000
   Bank B lent $6,400
   Bank C lent $5,120
   Total loans made so far $19,520
5. 1/reserve ratio = 1/0.20 = 5
6. Potential deposit creation = initial excess reserves x money multiplier = $8,000 x 5 = $40,000

CHAPTER 14

Monetary Policy

Quick Review

- The Federal Reserve System controls the money supply by limiting the amount of loans that the banking system can provide from any given level of reserves, and it also controls the amount of reserves in the system.

- The Federal Reserve System is comprised of twelve regional banks located in various regions of the country. The regional banks provide the following services for the private banks in their region: check clearing, holding bank reserves, providing currency, and providing loans to the private banks. The Board of Governors of the Federal Reserve System is the key decision maker in setting monetary policy. Board members are appointed by the president of the U.S. for fourteen-year terms.

- There are three primary levers of monetary policy: reserve requirements, discount rates, and open-market operations. Changing the reserve requirement changes both the money multiplier and the level of excess reserves in the banking system. It is the least frequently used tool.

- The process in which the Fed lends money to private banks is known as "discounting." Changing the discount rate makes it more or less attractive for private banks to borrow from the Fed.

- The principal monetary policy tool is open-market operations, which involves the buying or selling of government bonds in the open market by the Fed.

- The goal of monetary policy is to provide the appropriate level of aggregate demand (AD) in the economy to achieve our output, employment, and price level goals. Expansionary monetary policy shifts the AD curve to the right; restrictive policy shifts it to the left.

- The slope of the aggregate supply (AS) curve determines the impact of a given shift in AD. If AS is upward sloping then an increase in output is accompanied by an increase in the price level.

- Advocates of "discretionary" monetary policy argue that the Fed should be free to counter market instability by changing the growth rate of the money supply. Advocates of fixed "rules" believe the Fed should simply keep the money supply growing at a constant rate. They argue that the Fed itself is a source of instability!

Learning Objectives

After studying the chapter and doing the following exercises, you should:

1. Be familiar with the organization, structure, purposes, and functions of the Federal Reserve System.
2. Know how the reserve requirement can be changed to achieve a money-supply objective.
3. Know how the discount rate can be changed to achieve a given policy objective.
4. Know how the Fed can achieve a given policy objective by buying or selling securities.
5. Understand how the Fed's open-market activities alter portfolio decisions of market participants.
6. Understand how expansionary and restrictive monetary policy can be used to influence aggregate demand.
7. Understand how the slope of the aggregate supply curve determines the tradeoff between output and price level, which results from a given policy initiative.
8. Be able to discuss the "rules versus discretion" controversy.

Using Key Terms

Fill in the puzzle on the opposite page with the appropriate term from the list of Terms to Remember on page 316 in the text.

Across

3. The most frequently used monetary policy tool.
4. The curve affected by monetary policy in Figure 14.5 in the text.
6. The Federal Reserve System can use its powers to alter the _____.
8. Reduced by the Fed to stimulate economic growth according to the article on page 306 in the text.
9. Used by the Bank of Japan in the article on page 304 in the text to stimulate the macroeconomy.
10. Held by banks either as vault cash or as deposits at the regional Federal Reserve bank.

Down

1. Drawn with three different shapes in Figure 14.6 in the text.
2. Equal to 4 when the reserve ratio is equal to 25 percent.
5. The process by which private banks borrow reserves directly from the Fed.
7. Normally kept at a minimum except during the Great Depression according to Figure 14.3 in the text.

True or False: *Circle your choice and explain why any false statements are incorrect.*

T　　F　　1. The Federal Reserve's control over the money supply is the key mechanism of monetary policy.

T　　F　　2. Monetary policy affects aggregate supply.

T　　F　　3. The Fed is not one bank but is actually twelve regional banks with central control located in Washington D.C.

T　　F　　4. Banks typically hold their required reserves in their vaults.

T　　F　　5. If the Fed wishes to increase the money supply, it can reduce the discount rate.

T　　F　　6. Profit-maximizing banks try to keep their excess reserves as high as possible.

T　　F　　7. By buying bonds, the Fed decreases the quantity of transactions deposits in the banking system and reduces the quantity of loans.

T　　F　　8. The effectiveness of monetary policy depends solely on its ability to shift aggregate demand.

T　　F　　9. Restrictive policy is most effective when the aggregate supply curve is horizontal.

T　　F　　10. Proponents of fixed rules for monetary policy base their position on the assumption that the aggregate supply curve is vertical.

Multiple Choice: *Select the correct answer.*

_B_　1. The formulation of general Federal Reserve policy is the responsibility of the:
   (a) Federal Open Market Committee.
   (b) Board of Governors.
   (c) Federal Advisory Council.
   (d) Regional Federal Reserve banks.

_A_　2. Which of the following serves as the central banker for private banks in the United States?
   (a) The 12 regional Federal Reserve banks.
   (b) The Executive Branch of the government.
   (c) The Board of Governors of the Federal Reserve System.
   (d) The Federal Open Market Committee.

_B_　3. Suppose that Brian receives a check for $100 from a bank in Atlanta. He deposits the check in his account at his Baltimore bank. Brian's Baltimore bank will collect the $100 from the:
   (a) Atlanta bank.
   (b) Baltimore bank's regional Federal Reserve Bank.
   (c) The central Federal Reserve Bank in Washington.
   (d) Board of Governors.

_C_ 4. Members of the Federal Reserve Board of Governors are appointed for one fourteen-year term so that they:
   (a) Have time to learn how the Fed operates.
   (b) Are more likely to make politically acceptable decisions.
   (c) Make their decisions based on economic, rather than political, considerations.
   (d) Both a and b.

_D_ 5. Which of the following is a service performed by the Federal Reserve banks?
   (a) Clearing checks between commercial banks.
   (b) Holding reserves of commercial banks.
   (c) Providing currency to commercial banks.
   (d) All of the above.

_A_ 6. Which of the following is *not* one of the tools of monetary policy used by the Fed?
   (a) Expulsion from Fed membership.
   (b) Changing the reserve requirement.
   (c) Changing the discount rate.
   (d) Performing open-market operations.

_B_ 7. A change in the reserve requirement is the tool used least often by the Fed because:
   (a) It does not affect bank reserves.
   (b) It can cause abrupt changes in the money supply.
   (c) It does not affect the money multiplier.
   (d) It has no impact on the lending capacity of the banking system.

_A_ 8. Suppose that the banking system has total deposits of $20 billion, a reserve requirement of 20% and reserves of $4 billion. If the Fed lowers the reserve requirement to 10%, the money supply could potentially increase by as much as:
   (a) $20 billion.
   (b) $10 billion.
   (c) $40 billion.
   (d) $200 billion.

_B_ 9. Suppose that the Fed increases excess reserves in the banking system by $2 billion by buying $2 billion worth of bonds. Assuming the reserve requirement is 20%, the money supply could potentially increase by as much as:
   (a) $2 billion.
   (b) $10 billion.
   (c) $20 billion.
   (d) $400 million.

_B_ 10. Refer to the article in the text titled "Japanese Central Bank Cuts Reserve Requirements." Additional levers that would allow the Bank of Japan to achieve expansionary monetary policy include:
   (a) Selling bonds.
   (b) Reducing the discount rate.
   (c) Reducing personal income taxes.
   (d) All of the above are expansionary monetary policies.

191

_C_ 11. If the Fed wanted to reduce the money supply, it could:
  (a) Lower the discount rate.
  (b) Decrease the minimum reserve ratio.
  (c) Sell bonds.
  (d) All of the above would reduce the money supply.

_A_ 12. When the Fed wishes to increase the excess reserves of the member banks, it:
  (a) Buys securities.
  (b) Raises the discount rate.
  (c) Raises the reserve requirement.
  (d) Sells securities.

_D_ 13. When the Fed raises the discount rate, this policy:
  (a) Raises the cost of borrowing from the Fed.
  (b) Is a signal that the Fed is moving toward a more restrictive monetary policy.
  (c) Is an indication that the Fed is concerned about inflation.
  (d) Does all of the above.

_A_ 14. The monetarist aggregate supply curve is:
  (a) Perfectly vertical at the natural rate of unemployment.
  (b) Upward-sloping to the right.
  (c) Flat until full employment is reached.
  (d) Flat.

_C_ 15. Refer to Figure 14.5 in the text. The shift in aggregate demand from AD_1 to AD_2 could have been caused by:
  (a) Fiscal policy only.
  (b) An increase in the reserve requirement.
  (c) Expansionary monetary policy.
  (d) Fed sales of securities.

_B_ 16. The policy lever most commonly used by the Fed is:
  (a) Changes in the discount rate.
  (b) Buying and selling securities.
  (c) Changes in the reserve requirement.
  (d) Foreign-exchange operations.

_D_ 17. Expansionary monetary policy will:
  (a) Increase bank lending capacity.
  (b) Lower interest rates.
  (c) Encourage people to borrow and spend more money.
  (d) Do all of the above.

_D_ 18. An increase in the money supply will:
  (a) Always cause inflation.
  (b) Never causes inflation.
  (c) Cause inflation only if aggregate supply is horizontal.
  (d) Cause inflation if aggregate supply is upward sloping.

192

C

19. The natural rate of unemployment implies that in the long run:
    (a) The rate of unemployment can be permanently reduced by more expansionary monetary and fiscal policies.
    (b) The Federal Reserve can bring the economy to equilibrium by altering the money supply.
    (c) Monetary policy only affects the rate of inflation.
    (d) Discretionary monetary policy affects output.

D 20. Monetary policy is most effective against unemployment when lending capacity is:
    (a) Not fully utilized and aggregate supply is vertical.
    (b) Not fully utilized and aggregate supply is horizontal.
    (c) Fully utilized and aggregate supply is vertical.
    (d) Fully utilized and aggregate supply is horizontal.

Problems and Applications

The three exercises below demonstrate how monetary policy might work in a hypothetical situation.

Exercise 1

This exercise is similar to the problems at the end of the chapter in the text. The focus of this exercise is the reserve requirement.

Suppose the Fed wishes to expand M1. Carefully read the assumptions below and then work through the exercise step by step to achieve the policy objective. Assume:
- The banks in the system have initially $240 million of transactions account liabilities.
- The banking system has initially no excess reserves.
- The initial reserve requirement is 0.25.
- The banks make loans in the full amount of any excess reserves that they acquire.
- All loans flow back into the banking system as transactions accounts.

The combined balance sheet of the banks in the system is as shown in Table 14.1.

Table 14.1. Balance sheet of banking system when reserve requirement is 0.25 (millions of dollars)

Assets		Liabilities	
Total reserves	$ 60	Transactions accounts	$240
Required, $60			
Excess, $0			
Securities	80		
Loans	100		
Total	$240	Total	$240

1. Suppose the Fed lowers the reserve requirement to 0.20. How many dollars of excess reserves does this create? $ _____.

2. How large are required reserves now? $ _____.

3. How large are total reserves now? $ _____.

4. What is the additional lending capacity of the banking system due to the change in the reserve requirement from 0.25 to 0.20? $ _____.

5. Reconstruct the balance sheet in Table 14.2 to show the new totals for the accounts affected in the banking system because of the loans generated in Question 4 above.

**Table 14.2. Balance sheet of banking system when reserve requirement is 0.20
(millions of dollars)**

Assets		Liabilities	
Total reserves	$_____	Transactions accounts	$_____
Required, _____			
Excess, _____			
Securities	_____		
Loans	_____		_____
Total	$_____	Total	$_____

6. The money supply (M1) has expanded by $ _____.
7. Total reserves have increased by $ _____.
8. Loans have increased by $ _____.

Exercise 2

Like the problem at the end of the chapter in the text, this exercise shows how the money supply can be changed. The focus of this exercise is open-market policy.

Suppose the Fed purchases of $10 million of government securities in the open market.
Suppose further that:
- The banking system initially has no excess reserves.
- The reserve requirement is 0.20.
- The banks make loans in the full amount of any excess reserves that they acquire.
- All loans flow back into the banking system as transactions accounts.

Table 14.3. Balance sheet of banking system (millions of dollars)

Assets		Liabilities	
Total reserves	$ 60	Transactions accounts	$300
Required, $60			
Excess, $0			
Securities	80		
Loans	160		
Total	$300	Total	$300

1. Suppose the banking system now expands its loans and transactions accounts by the maximum amount it can on the basis of its $_____ in excess reserves.

2. In Table 14.4 complete the balance sheet for the banking system showing the new totals for all of the accounts after loans have been made. (*Remember:* The reserve ratio is 0.20.)

**Table 14.4. Balance sheet of banking system
after expansion of loans and deposits (millions of dollars)**

Assets		Liabilities	
Total reserves	$_____	Transactions accounts	$_____
Required, _____			
Excess, _____			
Securities	_____		
Loans	_____		
Total	$_____	Total	$_____

3. As a result of the open-market operations, the money supply has expanded by a total of $ _____.

4. Total reserves have increased by $ _____.

5. Loans have increased by $ _____.

Exercise 3

This exercise examines what might happen if the Fed were to decide to increase the discount rate.

1. An increase in the discount rate will cause M1 to (increase, decrease, stay the same).

2. This change in the money supply will cause aggregate (demand, supply) to shift to the (left, right).

3. What other actions could the Fed take to achieve the same impact on aggregate demand?

4. Suppose aggregate demand shifts to the left. Determine the change to the equilibrium price level and output level (increase or decrease) for each of the aggregate supply curve shapes in Table 14.5.

Table 14.5.

Aggregate supply curve	Change in price level	Change in output level
Upward sloping	_____	_____
Horizontal	_____	_____
Vertical	_____	_____

Exercise 4

Reread the Headline article in the text entitled "Italy Raises Interest Rates." Then answer the following questions.

1. Which interest rates did the central bank raise?

2. What sentence indicates the bank's reason for raising these key rates?

Common Errors

The first statement in each "common error" below is incorrect. Each incorrect statement is followed by a corrected version and an explanation.

1. Bank reserves are required for the safety of depositors' money. WRONG!
   Bank reserves are for control of the money supply. RIGHT!
      Many people have the idea that bank reserves provide for the safety of depositors' money. They don't. Reserves are for control of the money supply. The FDIC provides for safety of deposits by insuring them within limits. Reserves are not principally for depositors' safety.

2. Deposits of cash are necessary to start the process of lending and deposit creation. WRONG!
   To start the lending process, the banks must acquire reserves from outside of the banking system. RIGHT!
      Many find it difficult to understand that for deposit creation to occur, the banking system needs only to acquire reserves from outside the system. It may acquire reserves by selling a security to the Fed or by borrowing from the Fed. When an individual bank acquires reserves from another bank its reserves increase, but the other bank's reserves shrink. Thus, the system has no more reserves after the transaction than it had before, and so the system's lending capacity is unchanged.

■ ANSWERS ■

Using Key Terms

Across
3. open-market operations
4. aggregate demand
6. money supply
8. discount rate
9. monetary policy
10. required reserves

Down
1. aggregate supply
2. money multiplier
5. discounting
7. excess reserves

True or False

1. T
2. F   Monetary policy shifts the aggregate demand curve.
3. T
4. F   Banks hold the majority of required reserves in accounts at the regional Federal Reserve banks.
5. T
6. F   Unused excess reserves will not earn a return for the bank. Banks attempt to lend as much of their excess reserves as possible.
7. F   By buying bonds, the Fed is essentially taking bonds out of the hands of the public and replacing them with money thereby increasing both the quantity of transactions deposits and loans.
8. F   The effectiveness of monetary policy depends on its ability to shift aggregate demand and the shape of the AS curve.
9. F   Restrictive monetary policy is most effective in reducing inflation when the aggregate supply curve is vertical.
10. T

Multiple Choice

1. b	5. d	9. b	13. d	17. d
2. a	6. a	10. b	14. a	18. d
3. b	7. b	11. c	15. c	19. c
4. c	8. a	12. a	16. b	20. d

Problems and Applications

Exercise 1

1. $12 million
2. $48 million
3. $60 million
4. $60 million

5. See Table 14.2 answer
6. $60 million
7. Zero
8. $60 million

Table 14.2 Answer (millions of dollars)

Assets		Liabilities	
Total reserves	$ 60	Transactions accounts	$300
Required $60			
Excess $0			
Securities	80		
Loans	160		
Total	$300	Total	$300

Exercise 2

1. $10 million

2. **Table 14.4 Answer (millions of dollars)**

Assets		Liabilities	
Total reserves	$ 70	Transactions accounts	$350
Required $70			
Excess $0			
Securities	70		
Loans	210		
Total	$350	Total	$350

3. $50 million
4. $10 million
5. $50 million

Exercise 3

1. Decrease
2. Demand, left
3. An open-market purchase of government securities or an increase in the reserve requirement.

4. **Table 14.5 Answer (millions of dollars)**

Aggregate supply curve	Change in price level	Change in output level
Upward sloping	decrease	decrease
Horizontal	no change	decrease
Vertical	decrease	no change

Exercise 4

1. The discount rate and the fixed-term advances.

2. "... it is determined to fight inflation aggressively..."

CHAPTER 15

Economic Growth

Quick Review

- Economic growth refers to increases in real GDP. Growth is desired by virtually every society because it provides for possible improvements in the standard of living. In the short run, economic growth can be achieved by increased capacity utilization, represented by a movement toward the production-possibilities curve. In the long run, growth requires an increase in capacity itself, represented by a rightward shift of the production-possibilities curve. This results in a rightward shift in the long-run aggregate supply curve as well

- GDP per capita is a basic measure of living standards. GDP per worker is a measure of productivity. Increases in productivity, rather than increases in the quantity of resources available, have been the primary source of U.S. economic growth in the past.

- The sources of productivity gains include improvements in the quality of labor, increased investment and resulting increases in the nation's capital stock, research and development expenditures, and improved management skills and techniques.

- Government policies play a role in fostering economic growth. Policies that encourage growth include education and training, immigration, and programs that promote investment and saving. All of these can lead to increases in both the quality and quantity of resources available.

- Continued economic growth is desirable as long as it brings a higher standard of living for a country and an increased ability to produce and consume goods and services that society desires.

- Budget deficits may reduce the level of economic growth through "crowding out." This is an issue if increased government spending, financed by borrowing, causes a reduction in the level of private investment. So macroeconomic policies should be evaluated in terms of their effect on long-run aggregate supply.

- Government regulation may also inhibit economic growth. Regulation of both factor and product markets tends to reduce supply and raise production costs.

Learning Objectives

After studying the chapter and doing the following exercise you should:

1. Know the difference between short-run and long-run limits on economic growth.
2. Know that economic growth (decline) is measured using real GDP and be able to calculate the growth rate.
3. Understand why real GDP per capita is the common measure of living standards.
4. Understand that GDP per worker is used to measure productivity.
5. Be able to discuss the sources of productivity gains in the U.S. economy.
6. Know a variety of policy levers that can be used to facilitate the growth process.
7. Understand how (de)regulation and other types of government intervention affect factor and product markets.
8. Know when and how government's deficit spending imposes opportunity costs on society.

Using Key Terms

Fill in the puzzle on the opposite page with the appropriate term from the list of Terms to Remember on page 336 in the text.

Across

1. The actual quantity of goods and services produced, valued in constant prices.
4. Equal to $29,259 for the U.S. in 1997, according to the text.
7. All persons over the age of sixteen who are working for pay or looking for work.
8. This curve is used in Figure 15.1 to demonstrate long-run growth.
11. Calculated as –0.7 percent between 1990 and 1991 for the U.S. on page 322 in the text.

Down

2. Shown in Figure 15.1b as a rightward shift in the production-possibilities curve.
3. Increased by 3.1 percent a year for the U.S. during the 1980s according to Figure 15.4 in the text.
5. The U.S. _____ rate is far below that in most other countries according to the article on page 332 in the text.
6. A decrease in private-sector borrowing, and investment, because of increased government borrowing.
9. The current dollar value of output produced within a country's border.
10. A determinant of GDP growth according the article on page 327 in the text.

Puzzle 15.1

True or False: *Circle your choice and explain why any false statements are incorrect.*

T (F) 1. World economic growth has virtually eliminated poverty in most of the world.

T (F) 2. When an economy moves from a point inside its production-possibilities curve to a point on the curve, potential GDP has increased.

(T) F 3. An economy will be able to attain a combination of goods and services outside of its production-possibilities curve only by increasing its productive capacity.

T (F) 4. An increase in nominal GDP means that there has been an outward shift of the production-possibilities curve.

(T) F 5. A major goal of short-run economic policy is to produce a combination of goods and services on the production-possibilities curve.

T (F) 6. A shift of the production-possibilities curve outward corresponds to an increase in aggregate demand.

(T) F 7. Long-run economic policy attempts to shift the production-possibilities curve outward.

(T) F 8. Increased capital investment is possible only if consumption is reduced, that is saving increases.

T (F) 9. Overall, immigration has had a negative impact on the U.S. economy over time.

(T) F 10. Deregulation can lead to an increase in the aggregate supply curve by lowering production costs.

Multiple Choice: *Select the correct answer.*

B 1. When an economy is producing inside its production possibilities curve, it is an indication that:
   (a) There are not enough resources available to reach the production possibilities curve.
   (b) More output could be produced with existing resources.
   (c) The level of technology is limiting the level of production.
   (d) All of the above are correct.

C 2. In order to produce a combination of goods and services outside of the current production-possibilities curve, an economy would have to:
   (a) Use more of their existing resources.
   (b) Raise the prices of goods and services so that firms would produce more.
   (c) Find more resources, for example, for such a combination to be possible.
   (d) They will never be able to produce a combination of goods and services outside their current production-possibilities curve.

_B_ 3. A major goal of short-run macroeconomic policy is to:
(a) Shift the production-possibilities curve outward.
(b) Move toward the production-possibilities curve.
(c) Shift the aggregate demand curve to the left.
(d) Shift the aggregate supply curve to the left.

_A_ 4. Economic growth in the long run:
(a) Shifts the production-possibilities curve outward.
(b) Moves the economy along the production-possibilities curve.
(c) Moves the economy on to the production-possibilities curve.
(d) Shifts the aggregate supply curve to the left.

_A_ 5. When the production-possibilities curve shifts outward, we can also be sure that:
(a) Aggregate supply has increased.
(b) Output has increased.
(c) GDP per capita has increased.
(d) All of the above occur when the production-possibilities curve shifts outward.

_A_ 6. Real GDP is better than nominal GDP in making comparisons of GDP over time because:
(a) Nominal GDP can increase simply because of price increases.
(b) Real GDP is not affected by output changes.
(c) Nominal GDP is the hypothetical output that would be produced at full employment.
(d) Real GDP is not affected by changes in productivity or the size of the labor force.

_D_ 7. Whenever nominal GDP increases:
(a) Living standards improve.
(b) Output increases.
(c) The production-possibilities curve shifts outward.
(d) The value of production increases.

_C_ 8. Suppose that real GDP in an economy is expected to increase at a consistent 6 percent annually in the future. Use the "rule of 72" to estimate how many years it will take for production to double.
(a) 6 years.
(b) 10 years.
(c) 12 years.
(d) 72 years.

_D_ 9. Growth in GDP per capita is attained only when:
(a) There is growth in population.
(b) There is growth in output.
(c) Population is held constant.
(d) The growth in output exceeds population growth.

_C_ 10. Which of the following is the best measure of living standards in an economy?
(a) GDP per worker.
(b) Nominal GDP.
(c) GDP per capita.
(d) Population growth.

_D_ 11. In most less developed countries GDP per capita is declining because:
   (a) GDP is declining.
   (b) Population growth is negative.
   (c) Capital investment is zero.
   (d) Population growth is greater than the growth in GDP.

_D_ 12. Which of the following would likely contribute to an improvement in the productivity of labor?
   (a) Greater expenditures on training and education.
   (b) Improved management.
   (c) Greater expenditure on research and development.
   (d) All of the above.

_C_ 13. According to the text, which of the following has been most responsible for the increases in productivity in the United States since 1929?
   (a) Increases in the quantity of labor.
   (b) Increases in the amount of capital per worker.
   (c) Research and development.
   (d) Worker training.

_B_ 14. More technically advanced capital makes its contribution to productivity by:
   (a) Replacing labor.
   (b) Enhancing labor productivity.
   (c) Increasing profits for producers.
   (d) Increasing nominal GDP.

_A_ 15. Which of the following series of annual GDP growth rates would result in the highest level of GDP in ten years?
   (a) A constant 4 percent annual rate of growth.
   (b) Annual rates of 8 percent, 0 percent, 8 percent, 0 percent, etc. for ten years.
   (c) Annual rates of 6 percent, −6 percent, 6 percent, −6 percent, etc. for ten years.
   (d) All of these patterns of growth would result in the same level of GDP after ten years.

_D_ 16. Which of the following is a source of productivity increase?
   (a) Research and development.
   (b) Improvements in labor quality.
   (c) Capital investment.
   (d) All of the above.

_D_ 17. Which of the following can have an impact on the aggregate supply curve?
   (a) Immigration policies.
   (b) Minimum-wage laws.
   (c) Tax treatment of capital gains.
   (d) All of the above.

_B_ 18. Which of the following policies is most likely to increase the aggregate supply curve?
   (a) More strict occupational safety regulations.
   (b) A cut in the capital gains tax.
   (c) Raising the minimum wage.
   (d) All of the above would cause aggregate supply to increase.

19. Which of the following statements is true regarding the "crowding out" effect?
    (a) It results in a diversion of available saving from business investment to government spending.
    (b) It always acts as a constraint on economic growth.
    (c) It occurs at any point in the business cycle.
    (d) All of the above are true.

20. The current problems in the U.S. of congested highways, poor air quality, and global warming are primarily the result of:
    (a) Too many goods and services.
    (b) The mix of output produced.
    (c) Too much government regulation.
    (d) Excessively high levels of GDP per capita.

Problems and Applications

Exercise 1

The following exercise shows how gross domestic product can be used to indicate the standard of living and the rate of economic growth in an economy.

1. Using the data provided complete Table 15.1.

Table 15.1

	1970	1990	Percentage change
(1) U.S. real GDP (billions of dollars)	$3388.2	$6138.7	_____
(2) U.S. population (thousands)	205,052	249,924	_____
(3) U.S. per capita GDP (dollars per person)	$16,524	$24,562	_____
(4) World population (thousands)	3,722,000	5,329,000	_____

2. Using the information in Table 15.1, the U.S. standard of living (increased, decreased) from 1970 to 1990.

3. Why must the world economic growth be greater than the U.S. economic growth to maintain the same standard of living? _____

4. From 1970 to 1990, what was the average annual growth rate for real GDP in the U.S? _____

5. If the growth rate calculated in Question 4 was the actual growth rate each year (not the average), how long should it take for real GDP to double according to Table 15.1 in the text? _____

Exercise 2

The focus of this exercise is the value of investment in spurring economic growth. This exercise will help you with the second problem at the end of Chapter 15.

Suppose that every additional five percentage points in the investment rate (I/GDP) boosts economic growth by two percentage points. Assume also that all investment must be financed with household saving. Suppose the economy is currently characterized by the following data:

GDP:	$5 trillion
Consumption:	4 trillion
Saving:	1 trillion
Investment:	1 trillion

1. What is the current investment rate (I/GDP)? _____

2. If the goal is to raise the growth rate of income by one percentage point, by how much must investment increase? _____

3. By how much must consumption decline to permit the necessary growth in the investment rate to reach the 1% target? _____

4. How much does income increase in the first year due to the 1% growth rate? _____

5. Assuming that income each year in the future is 1% higher as a result of the one-year change in the investment rate, how many years will it take for the economy to recoup the amount of consumption goods given up to finance the increase in investment? _____

Exercise 3

Reread the Headline article in the text entitled "Labor Supply" and answer the following questions.

1. Is immigration a help or a hindrance to the long-term economic growth of the United States?

2. What changes are required in immigration policy so that immigrants can improve the prospects for economic growth?

Common Errors

The first statement in the "common error" below is incorrect. The incorrect statement is followed by a corrected version and an explanation.

1. Labor productivity increases when more output is produced per dollar of wages. WRONG!
   Labor productivity increases when more units of product are produced per unit of labor. RIGHT!
   Productivity changes are not directly related to wage levels. Wage levels reflect a large number of influences embodied in the demand and supply curves for labor. Productivity, however, is a physical measure of the relationship between units of product and the amount of labor needed to produce the product.

■ ANSWERS ■

Using Key Terms

Across

1. real GDP
4. GDP per capita
7. labor force
8. production possibilities
11. growth rate

Down

2. economic growth
3. productivity
5. saving
6. crowding out
9. nominal GDP
10. investment

True or False

1. F Over half of the world's population lives in poverty.
2. F Potential GDP increases only when the production-possibilities curve shifts outward.
3. T
4. F Changes in nominal GDP do not tell us anything about either changes in production or productive capacity because nominal GDP does not adjust for changing prices.
5. T
6. F A shift of the production-possibilities curve outward corresponds to an increase in aggregate supply.
7. T
8. T
9. F Immigration has significantly increased the labor force and contributed to the outward shift of the U.S. production-possibilities curve over time.
10. T

Multiple Choice

1. b	5. a	9. d	13. c	17. d
2. c	6. a	10. c	14. b	18. b
3. b	7. d	11. d	15. a	19. a
4. a	8. c	12. d	16. d	20. b

Problems and Applications

Exercise 1

1. **Table 15.1 Answer**

	1970	1990	Percentage change
(1) U.S. real GDP (billions of dollars)	$3388.2	$6138.7	81.2%
(2) U.S. population (thousands)	205,052	249,924	21.9%
(3) U.S. per capita GDP (dollars per person)	$16,524	$24,562	48.6%
(4) World population (thousands)	3,722,000	5,329,000	43.2%

2. Increased
3. Since the world population growth rate is faster than that of the U.S., it takes higher economic growth to maintain the same standard of living.
4. 4.06%
5. 18 years

Exercise 2

1. I/GDP is $1 trillion/$5 trillion = 0.20 or 20%.
2. To raise the income level by 1 percent the I/GDP ratio must rise by 2.5 percent.
   0.25 x $5 trillion = $0.125 trillion or $125 billion.
3. Saving must rise by the same amount ($0.125 trillion) as investment increases, so consumption must fall by that amount as well.
4. One percent of $5 trillion is $50 billion.
5. $0.125 trillion is $125 billion. $125 billion divided by 50 billion is 2.5. It will take two and a half years to recoup the lost consumption.

Exercise 3

1. The article notes that "U.S. sorely needs immigrant talent to compensate for the shrinking birthrate ... and to replenish the stagnating pool of skilled labor."

2. Immigration policy must be changed to favor those who possess the skills that are in short supply in the U.S., thus following the example of Australia and Canada.

CHAPTER 16

Theory and Reality

Quick Review

- Government policy makers have many tools with which to design and implement the ideal "package" of macro policies.

- The basic tools of fiscal policy are taxes and government spending. Automatic stabilizers such as income taxes and unemployment benefits help to stabilize any disruptions in the economy by responding automatically to changes in national income.

- Monetary policy, controlled by the Federal Reserve, uses open market operations, changes in the discount rate, and occasional changes in the reserve requirement to impact the macroeconomy. Both monetary and fiscal policy shift the aggregate demand curve.

- Supply-side policy focuses on shifting the aggregate supply curve, which allows for economic growth. Tax cuts, government deregulation, education, training, and research are supply-side tools.

- To end a recession, we can cut taxes, expand the money supply, or increase government spending. To curb inflation, we can reverse each of these policy levers. To overcome stagflation, fiscal and monetary policies can be combined with supply-side incentives.

- Recurring economic slowdowns with accompanying increases in unemployment and nagging inflation suggest that obstacles may stand in the way of successful policy making. In addition, there are opportunity costs for all policy decisions, and economic goals may even conflict one another.

- Measurement problems exist because data is always dated and incomplete, and we must rely on forecasts of future economic activity that have an inherent accuracy problem. Design problems exist as well because we are frequently unsure of just how the economy will respond to specific policy initiatives. Implementation problems reflect the time it takes Congress and the president to agree on an appropriate plan of action. And there is always the chance that policy approaches will reflect political needs rather than economic needs.

- Those who favor discretionary policies believe that active intervention is necessary. Others, who believe fine-tuning is not possible, favor fixed policy rules.

Learning Objectives

After studying the chapter and doing the following exercises you should:

1. Know the three basic types of economic policy and the policy levers for each.
2. Be able to describe the basic policies to fight recession, deal with inflation, and eliminate stagflation.
3. Know the record of policy makers in controlling unemployment and inflation and in achieving economic growth.
4. Understand how goal conflicts, and measurement, design, and implementation problems affect policy making.
5. Understand the debate over rules versus discretion in policy making.

Using Key Terms

Fill in the puzzle on the opposite page with the appropriate term from the list of Terms to Remember on page 359 in the text.

Across

1. Alternating periods of expansion and contraction in the economy.
3. Government spending and receipts that occur because of a change in the business cycle.
5. Begins on October 1 for the U.S. federal government.
6. The attempt to correct even small changes in the macroeconomy.
7. Equal to $1/(1-MPC)$.
10. The goal of _____ is to increase aggregate supply.
11. The Federal Reserve uses monetary policy tools to change the _____.
12. The situation shown in Figure 16.1 in the text.

Down

2. Occurs because of the mismatch between worker's skills and the available jobs.
4. The use of open-market operations, discount-rate changes, and reserve requirements to change the macroeconomy.
8. The difference between full-employment GDP and equilibrium GDP.
9. The use of government spending and taxes to change the macroeconomy.

Puzzle 16.1

True or False: *Circle your choice and explain why any false statements are incorrect.*

T   F   1. The failure of macroeconomic policy is reflected in the fact that since World War II, the ups and downs of the business cycle have become more severe.

T   F   2. The federal budget contains the details of fiscal policy.

T   F   3. Automatic stabilizers tend to smooth out the business cycle.

T   F   4. The shape of the aggregate demand curve is the most important determinant of the effectiveness of fiscal and monetary policy.

T   F   5. Good economic policy and political objectives often conflict.

T   F   6. President Clinton's "Rebuild America" program was essentially a supply-side policy.

T   F   7. Stagflation is caused by a decrease in aggregate demand.

T   F   8. "Fine-tuning" the economy is a generally accepted approach to macro policy because time lags in implementation are not a problem.

T   F   9. The Fed has traditionally been willing to sacrifice price stability in order to achieve low levels of unemployment.

T   F   10. Macroeconomic forecasts from different computer models are usually surprisingly similar because the models are based on the same macroeconomic theories.

Multiple Choice: *Select the correct answer.*

_D_   1. Which of the following is an accurate statement concerning the performance of macroeconomic policy in the United States?
(a) We have frequently failed to reach our goals of full employment, price stability, and vigorous economic growth.
(b) The business cycle continues to exist.
(c) The ups and downs of the business cycle have been less severe since World War II.
(d) All of the above are accurate.

_C_   2. The Balanced Budget and Taxpayer Relief Acts of 1997 provided:
(a) A fiscal stimulus to the economy.
(b) Fiscal restraint to the economy.
(c) A combination of fiscal stimulus and restraint.
(d) A monetary policy stimulus to the economy.

_A_   3. As the economy grows out of a recession, automatic stabilizers cause:
(a) Smaller budget deficits.
(b) Government spending to increase.
(c) The money supply to increase.
(d) Tax revenues to be reduced.

A   4. Which of the following is an example of fiscal policy?
(a) The Balanced Budget Act of 1997.
(b) Deregulation of financial institutions.
(c) Changes in immigration law.
(d) Changes in the money supply.

B   5. Fiscal and monetary policy are most effective in reducing inflation when the:
(a) Aggregate supply curve is horizontal.
(b) Aggregate supply curve is vertical.
(c) Aggregate supply is upward sloping but not vertical.
(d) Aggregate demand curve is vertical.

A   6. Which of the following is considered an appropriate policy by a Neo-Keynesian during a recession?
(a) Expand the money supply and increase government spending.
(b) Expand the money supply and decrease government spending.
(c) Contract the money supply and increase government spending.
(d) Contract the money supply and decrease government spending.

B   7. Expansionary fiscal and monetary policy are not effective in increasing the level of output when the:
(a) Aggregate supply curve is horizontal.
(b) Aggregate supply curve is vertical.
(c) Aggregate supply is upward sloping but not vertical.
(d) Aggregate demand curve is vertical.

B   8. Refer to the article titled "Policy Adjustments" in the text. When the Fed raises interest rates they are attempting to:
(a) Increase aggregate demand.
(b) Decrease aggregate demand.
(c) Increase aggregate supply.
(d) Decrease aggregate supply.

C   9. Refer to Table 16.3 in the text. Fed policy during this period can be described as:
(a) Consistently expansionary.
(b) Consistently restrictive.
(c) At times expansionary; at other times, restrictive.
(d) Following fixed rules.

C   10. Which of the following is an accurate statement about supply-side policy?
(a) The aggregate supply curve should be shifted to the right during periods of inflation and to the left during a recession.
(b) The aggregate supply curve should be shifted to the left during periods of inflation and to the right during a recession.
(c) The aggregate supply curve should be shifted to the right during periods of both inflation and recession.
(d) The aggregate supply curve should be left alone.

_D_ 11. Supply-side policy is designed to:
- (a) Move the economy from a point inside the production-possibilities curve to a point on it, and shift the aggregate supply curve to the left.
- (b) Move the economy from a point inside the production-possibilities curve to a point on it, and shift the aggregate supply curve to the right.
- (c) Shift the production-possibilities curve outward and shift the aggregate supply curve to the left.
- (d) Shift the production-possibilities curve outward and shift the aggregate supply curve to the right.

_D_ 12. Which of the following is the Monetarist policy for fighting a recession?
- (a) Increase government spending.
- (b) Expand the money supply at a faster rate.
- (c) Provide tax incentives to increase investment.
- (d) Patience (i.e., laissez-faire).

_A_ 13. Which of the following could be both a supply-side and a fiscal policy tool during a recession?
- (a) Tax cuts.
- (b) Deregulation.
- (c) Worker training programs.
- (d) Liberalized immigration laws.

_C_ 14. Which of the following would be recommended by Supply-siders to fight stagflation?
- (a) Raise tax rates.
- (b) Increase the money supply.
- (c) Deregulation.
- (d) Increase government expenditure.

_D_ 15. Which of the following is a reason that many economic policies fail?
- (a) Measurement difficulties prevent policy makers from correctly identifying what is happening in the economy.
- (b) Forecasts may be inaccurate.
- (c) There are lags in response to policies.
- (d) All of the above.

_B_ 16. Many economists argue that the CPI overstates inflation by two to three percentage points. From the point of view of those designing economic policy, this is an example of:
- (a) A goal conflict.
- (b) A measurement problem.
- (c) A design problem.
- (d) An implementation problem.

_A_ 17. The problem of deciding whether to provide aid to foreign countries when there are unreolved problems at home is an example of:
- (a) A goal conflict.
- (b) A measurement problem.
- (c) A design problem.
- (d) An implementation problem.

18. The time it takes for Congress to deliberate over fiscal policy is an example of:
- (a) A goal conflict.
- (b) A measurement problem.
- (c) A design problem.
- (d) An implementation problem.

19. The political business cycle refers to:
- (a) The ups and downs in overall business activity.
- (b) The political independence of the Fed's Board of Governors.
- (c) The concept of politicians stimulating the economy before an election, then tightening fiscal policy afterward.
- (d) Illegal behavior on the part of politicians.

20. Advocates of fixed policy rules believe:
- (a) That dicsretionary policies can improve macro outcomes.
- (b) Appropriate macro policy would include constant increases in the money supply and balanced federal budgets.
- (c) That because of the many problems associated with implementing fiscal and monetary policy, the economy would be better off if discretionary policy were abandoned.
- (d) All of the above.

Problems and Applications

Exercise 1

This exercise will help you recognize the inherent tradeoffs in the economy.

Table 16.1 presents data on interest rates, government expenditures, taxes, exports, imports, investment, consumption, a price index, unemployment, and pollution for four levels of equilibrium income (GDP). These items appear frequently in newspaper articles about the economy.

Table 16.1. Level of key economic indicators, by GDP level (billions of dollars per year)

Interest rate	30%	20%	10%	0%
Government expenditures	$100	$100	$100	$100
Taxes	$ 25	$ 75	$125	$175
Budget balance	$_____	$_____	$_____	$_____
Exports	$300	$300	$300	$300
Imports	$260	$280	$300	$320
Investment	$ 10	$ 90	$170	$250
Consumption	$750	$790	$830	$870
Nominal GDP	$_____	$_____	$_____	$_____
Price index	1.00	1.00	1.02	1.10
Real GDP (constant dollars)	$_____	$_____	$_____	$_____
Unemployment rate	15%	7%	4%	3.5%

1. Compute the federal budget balance, nominal GDP, and real GDP in Table 16.1, for the four different economic situations.
   (*Hint:* Remember the formula $C + I + G + [X - M] = $ GDP.)

2. Which policy is the government most likely using to reach each of the situations in Table 16.1?
   (a) Fiscal policy.
   (b) Monetary policy.
   (c) Wage and price controls.
   (d) Labor policy.

3. Which of the following statements best explains why the amount paid in taxes might change as the level of GDP changes in Table 16.1?
   (a) Taxpayers experience stagflation as income increases.
   (b) As taxpayers' incomes rise, their marginal tax rates rise.
   (c) The income tax is regressive.
   (d) Automatic stabilizers link taxes with income.

4. The reason that the price index changes as the level of GDP changes, as shown in Table 16.1, is most likely that as:
   (a) People receive greater income, they can be more discriminating buyers and find the lowest prices.
   (b) Firms receive more orders, productivity rises allowing inflation to ease.
   (c) People receive greater income, they spend it even when the economy is at full capacity, thus bidding up prices.
   (d) Businesses receive greater income, they have an incentive to expand capacity and must pass the cost of the increased capacity on to consumers in the form of higher prices.

5. The reason that unemployment changes as the level of GDP changes, as shown in Table 16.1, is most likely that as GDP rises:
   (a) People do not need jobs and leave the labor force.
   (b) Automatic stabilizers provide increased benefits to the unemployed, keeping them out of the labor force.
   (c) Inflation causes real income and employment to fall.
   (d) Aggregate demand rises, stimulating the derived demand for labor.

Exercise 2

This exercise shows the difficulties faced by policy makers because of the inevitable tradeoffs in the economy.

Table 16.2 presents data on government expenditure, taxes, exports, imports, a price index, unemployment, and pollution for four levels of equilibrium income (GDP). These items appear frequently in newspaper articles about the economy.

Table 16.2. Level of key economic indicators, by GDP level
(billions of dollars per year)

Indicator	Nominal GDP			
	$120	$160	$200	$240
Government expenditure	$ 0	$ 20	$ 35	$ 50
Taxes	$ 18	$ 24	$ 30	$ 36
Budget balance	$____	$____	$____	$____
Price index	1.00	1.00	1.02	1.20
Real GDP (constant dollars)	$____	$____	$____	$____
Unemployment rate	15%	7%	4%	3.5%
Pollution index	1.00	1.10	1.80	1.90

1. Compute the federal budget balance and real GDP in Table 16.2 for each level of nominal GDP.

2. Which government expenditure level would best accomplish all of the following goals according to Table 16.2? $ _____
   - Lowest taxes.
   - Lowest pollution.
   - Lowest inflation rate.

3. Which of the following might induce a policy maker to choose a higher government expenditure level than the one that answers Question 2?
   (a) High unemployment.
   (b) Government's inability to provide public goods and services.
   (c) Low real income.
   (d) All of the above.

4. Which government expenditure level would best accomplish all of the following goals?
   $ _____
   - Lowest unemployment rate.
   - Highest amount of government spending.
   - Highest real income.

5. The policy that best satisfies the goals in Question 4 would most likely result in:
   (a) A recession.
   (b) Rapid economic growth accompanied by inflation.
   (c) Stagflation.
   (d) None of the above.

6. Which government expenditure level would best accomplish all of the following goals?
   $ _____
   - Balancing the federal budget.
   - Maintaining pollution at reasonably low levels.
   - Maintaining price stability.

7. At which government expenditure level does full employment occur? (Use 4 percent unemployment as full employment.) $ _____

8. If you were a policy maker faced with the alternatives in Table 16.2, would you be able to say that one of the alternative government expenditure levels was clearly best? _____

Exercise 3

This exercise tests your ability to choose the appropriate policy initiative to overcome various undesirable economic conditions.

Choose a policy from the list below that would be appropriate to correct the economic conditions at the top of Table 16.3. Place the letter of each item only once in Table 16.3.

a. Deregulation.
b. Discount rate lowered.
c. Discount rate raised.
d. Government spending decreases.
e. Government spending increases.
f. Open-market operations (Fed buys government securities).
g. Open-market operations (Fed sells government securities).

h. Reserve requirement higher.
i. Reserve requirement lower.
j. Skill training and other labor market aids.
k. Tax cuts.
l. Tax incentives to alter the structure of supply and demand.
m. Tax incentives to encourage saving.
n. Tax increases.

Table 16.3. Economic policies

	Recession	Inflation	Stagflation
Fiscal policy	1._____	6._____	
	2._____	7._____	
Monetary policy	3._____	8._____	
	4._____	9._____	
	5._____	10._____	
Supply-side policy		11._____	12._____
			13._____
			14._____

Exercise 4

Reread the Headline article entitled "For Clinton, the Politics of a Tax Cut Are Sure to Clash with the Economics" in the text.

1. What is the "clash with the economics" that is referred to in the article?

2. Find the phrase indicating that the idea of a tax cut is as much politics as it is economics.

218

Common Errors

The first statement in each "common error" below is incorrect. Each incorrect statement is followed by a corrected version and an explanation.

1. Fiscal and monetary policies should be consistently applied to stimulate the economy. WRONG!

   Fiscal and monetary policies must be tailored to the specific economic problems faced by the economy. RIGHT!

   The government sometimes needs to apply apparently contradictory monetary and fiscal policies in order to pursue contradictory goals. For example, an expansionary fiscal policy may be needed to stimulate the economy, but a contractionary monetary policy may be needed to raise interest rates so that foreign capital will be attracted to U.S. financial markets. A policy maker must weigh tradeoffs and decide on the appropriate mix of policies.

2. Fiscal, monetary, and stagflation policies are effective regardless of the current income level of the economy. WRONG!

   The state of the economy in relation to full employment is important in determining the effectiveness of the various policies. RIGHT!

   Work force policies are often more effective in matching people with jobs when many people are looking for work than when unemployment is low. It is easier for the government to increase expenditures to stimulate the economy when there is a recession than to cut expenditures to fight inflation.

■ ANSWERS ■

Using Key Terms

Across
1. business cycle
3. automatic stabilizer
5. fiscal year
6. fine-tuning
7. multiplier
10. supply-side policy
11. money supply
12. stagflation

Down
2. structural unemployment
4. monetary policy
8. GDP gap
9. fiscal policy

True or False

1. F   The ups and downs of the business cycle have become less severe since World War II possibly indicating partial success.
2. T
3. T
4. F   The shape of the aggregate supply curve is the most important determinant of the effectiveness of fiscal and monetary policy.
5. T
6. T
7. F   Stagflation is caused by a decrease in aggregate supply.
8. F   "Fine-tuning" is not generally accepted because time lags in implementation are a problem (along with goal conflicts and measurement and design problems).
9. F   The Fed has traditionally emphasized price stability and has accepted higher levels of unemployment to achieve this goal.
10. F   Macroeconomic forecasts often differ because the models are based on different macroeconomic theories (e.g., Keynesian, supply-side).

Multiple Choice

1. d	5. b	9. c	13. a	17. a
2. c	6. a	10. c	14. c	18. d
3. a	7. b	11. d	15. d	19. c
4. a	8. b	12. d	16. b	20. d

Problems and Applications

Exercise 1

1. **Table 16.1 Answer (billions of dollars per year)**

Interest rate	30%	20%	10%	0%
Budget balance	$ –75	$ –25	$ 25	$ 75
Nominal GDP	$ 900	$ 1,000	$ 1,100	$ 1,200
Real GDP (constant dollars)	$ 900	$ 1,000	$ 1,078	$ 1,091

At the 30 percent interest rate, the following calculations should have been made, in billions of dollars per year:

Budget balance = $25 – $100 = $–75

Nominal GDP = $750 + $10 + $100 + $40 = $900

2. b   3. b   4. c   5. d

Exercise 2

1. **Table 16.2 Answer (billions of dollars per year)**

Indicator	Nominal GDP $120	$160	$200	$240
Budget balance	$ 18	$ 4	$ –5	$ –14
Real GDP (constant dollars)	$ 120	$ 160	$ 196	$ 200

2. $0   4. $50 billion   6. $20 billion   8. No

3. d   5. b   7. $35 billion

Exercise 3

Table 16.3 Answer

	Recession	Inflation	Stagflation
Fiscal	1. k Tax cuts 2. e Government spending increases	6. n Tax increases 7. d Government spending decreases	
Monetary policy	3. b Discount rate lowered 4. f Open-market operations (Fed buys government securities) 5. i Reserve requirement lower	8. c Discount rate raised 9. g Open-market operations (Fed sells government securities) 10. h Reserve requirement higher	
Supply-side policy		11. m Tax incentives to encourage saving	12. a Deregulation 13. l Tax incentives to alter the structure of supply and demand 14. j Skill training and other labor market aids

Exercise 4

1. The "clash" refers to paying for the tax cut with offsetting spending cuts.

2. "The case for a tax cut is simple: To boost the chances of reelection, Mr. Clinton needs to reshape his image and return to the themes that played well in 1992."

221

CHAPTER 17

International Trade

Quick Review

- The trade balance for any country is the difference between its exports and imports. Since the mid-1970s, the U.S. has experienced a trade deficit.

- Without trade, each country's consumption possibilities are limited to its production possibilities. With trade, a country may concentrate its resources on the goods it produces relatively efficiently. Trade allows for specialization and increases total world output. For each country, consumption possibilities will exceed production possibilities.

- For trade to be mutually beneficial each country must exploit its comparative advantage. Comparative advantage is based on relative efficiency in production. If Country A produces a specific good and in doing so gives up less in terms of other goods than Country B gives up to produce the same good, then Country A has a comparative advantage. Comparative advantage relies on a comparison of relative opportunity costs.

- For trade to be mutually beneficial, the terms of trade—the rate at which one good is exchanged for another—must lie between the opportunity costs for each of the individual countries. The closer the terms of trade are to the slope of a country's production-possibilities curve, the fewer benefits it receives, and vice versa.

- Not everyone benefits from trade. Those involved in import competing industries will object to trade because they may lose jobs to foreign producers. Those engaged in export industries will favor trade because jobs and profits are likely to increase. Trade adjustment assistance has sometimes been used to help those displaced by the forces of free trade.

- Tariffs discourage imports by making the goods more expensive. Quotas set a limit on the quantity of a particular good that may be imported. Voluntary restraint agreements (VRAs) limit the volume of trade and have the same impact as quotas.

Learning Objectives

After studying the chapter and doing the following exercises you should:

1. Know some basic facts about U.S. trade patterns.
2. Be able to calculate basic trade balances.
3. Understand why specialization and trade allow consumption possibilities to exceed production possibilities.
4. Be able to explain comparative advantage using opportunity costs.
5. Know how to determine the limits to the terms of trade.
6. Recognize the sources of pressure that result in restricted trade and the typical arguments used to justify doing so.
7. Be able to discuss tariffs, quotas, and currency devaluation as barriers to trade.
8. Understand how GATT and NAFTA support the idea of free trade.

Using Key Terms

Fill in the puzzle on the opposite page with the appropriate term from the list of Terms to Remember on page 386 in the text.

Across
3. Drawn in Figure 17.1 in the text for the U.S. and France.
5. Equal to a country's production possibilities without trade.
6. When a country's exports exceed its imports.
9. Equal to 11 percent of GDP for the U.S. according to the article on page 365 in the text.
11. Used to aid workers who lose their jobs when imported goods replace domestically produced goods.
12. An imbalance experienced by the U.S. since the mid-1970s.
13. The quantity of good A that must be given up in exchange for good B.
14. A tax on imported goods.
15. The price of one country's currency in terms of another country's currency.

Down
1. Determined by the intersection of demand and supply curves in Figure 17.3 in the text.
2. A quota placed by a country on its own exports.
4. May reduce sales, jobs, and profits in competing industries according to the article on page 375 in the text.
5. When the opportunity cost of producing a good is lower in one country than in another.
7. The quantity of one good that must be given up in order to produce one more unit of another good.
8. When a country can produce more of a good than another country with the same amount of resources.
10. Has a negative impact on domestic consumers and foreign producers according to the article on page 381 in the text.

True or False: *Circle your choice and explain why any false statements are incorrect.*

T F 1. The United States buys large quantities of goods and services from other countries but foreign countries buy very few of our goods and services.

T F 2. Since one country's imports are another country's exports, overall world trade must balance.

T F 3. When countries specialize, total world output increases.

T F 4. The main reason why countries specialize and trade with each other is so they can get goods and services they cannot produce themselves.

T F 5. It is impossible for a country to consume a mix of goods and services beyond its production-possibilities curve.

T F 6. A country has a comparative advantage in the production of a good when the output of the good per worker is higher than in any other country.

T F 7. In establishing the "terms of trade," a country will not give up more for a good in trade than it would give up if it produced the good itself.

T F 8. Everybody wins when countries specialize and trade.

T F 9. Compared to a free-trade situation, tariffs and quotas reduce world output and lower living standards.

T F 10. If the value of a nation's currency increases, *ceteris paribus*, its exports will decrease and its imports will increase.

Multiple Choice: *Select the correct answer.*

_____C_____ 1. Which of the following statements about U.S. trade is true?
  (a) Since the 1970s, foreign countries have bought more of our goods and services than we have bought from them.
  (b) The U.S. has a trade deficit with each of the countries it trades with.
  (c) The U.S. typically has a substantial trade surplus in services.
  (d) All of the above are true.

_____C_____ 2. Suppose the country of Montgomery has specialized in the production of a good but has not yet entered into a trade. At this point in time, Montgomery:
  (a) Has moved to a level of production outside its production-possibilities curve.
  (b) Has shifted its production-possibilities curve outward.
  (c) Has moved along its existing production-possibilities curve.
  (d) Has moved to a level of consumption outside its production-possibilities curve.

_D_   3. Referring back to the previous question, suppose that Montgomery now trades with another country. We can say that Montgomery:

(a) Has moved to a level of production outside its production-possibilities curve.
(b) Has shifted its production-possibilities curve outward.
(c) Has moved along its existing production-possibilities curve.
(d) Has moved to a level of consumption outside its production-possibilities curve.

_A_   4. World output of goods and services increases with specialization because:

(a) The world's resources are being used more efficiently.
(b) Each country's production-possibilities curve is shifted outward.
(c) Each country's workers are able to produce more than they could before specialization.
(d) All of the above are correct.

_B_   5. In the absence of trade, a country's consumption possibilities are:

(a) More than its domestic production possibilities.
(b) Equal to its domestic production possibilities.
(c) Less than its production possibilities.
(d) Unlimited, since the terms of trade are not a constraint.

_A_   6. "Absolute advantage" refers to:

(a) The ability of a country to produce a specific good with fewer resources than other countries can.
(b) The ability of a country to produce a specific good at a lower opportunity cost than its trading partners can.
(c) Total market domination by one country in the production a certain good or service.
(d) The ability of a country to guarantee itself very favorable terms of trade at the expense of its trading partners.

_C_   7. To say that a country has a comparative advantage in the production of wine is to say that:

(a) It can produce wine with fewer resources than any other country can.
(b) Its opportunity cost of producing wine is greater than any other country's.
(c) Its opportunity cost of producing wine is lower than any other country's.
(d) The relative price of wine is higher in that country than in any other.

Suppose the productivities of Japanese and U.S. producers are as indicated in Table 17.1. Refer to Table 17. in answering Questions 8-11.

Table 17.1. Output per worker-day in the United States and Japan

Country	TV sets (per day)	Bicycles (per day)
Japan	2	10
United States	1	8

_D_ 8. Which of the following statements is true?
- (a) The United States has an absolute advantage in the production of bicycles.
- (b) Japan has an absolute advantage in the production of bicycles only.
- (c) Japan has an absolute advantage in the production of TV sets only.
- (d) Japan has an absolute advantage in the production of both bicycles and TV sets.

_B_ 9. Which of the following is a true statement?
- (a) The opportunity cost of TV sets is higher in Japan than in the United States.
- (b) The opportunity cost of TV sets is lower in Japan than in the United States.
- (c) It is impossible to tell anything about opportunity cost from the information given.
- (d) The United States has a comparative advantage in the production of TV sets.

_A_ 10. Which of the following statements is true?
- (a) The U.S. should specialize in the production of bicycles and import TV sets from Japan.
- (b) The U.S. should specialize in the production of TV sets and import bicycles from Japan.
- (c) The U.S. should import both bicycles and TV sets from Japan.
- (d) The U.S. cannot compete with Japan; protectionist trade barriers should be implemented.

_C_ 11. Which of the following statements is true concerning the terms of trade between the U.S. and Japan?
- (a) The U.S. should not give up more than 1/8 of a bicycle to get one TV set.
- (b) The U.S. should not give up more than 10 bicycles to get one TV set.
- (c) The U.S. should not give up more than 8 bicycles to get one TV set.
- (d) The U.S. should not give up more than 1/5 of a bicycle to get one TV set.

_D_ 12. With regard to international trade, the market mechanism:
- (a) Provides a profit incentive to producers who specialize in the goods and services for which a comparative advantage exists.
- (b) Provides a profit incentive to producers who trade in the goods and services for which a comparative advantage exists.
- (c) Determines the terms of trade.
- (d) Does all of the above.

_A,D_ 13. Suppose that Brazil has a comparative advantage in coffee and Mexico has a comparative advantage in tomatoes. Which two of the following groups would be worse off if these two countries specialize and trade?
- (a) Brazilian tomato producers.
- (b) Brazilian coffee producers.
- (c) Mexican tomato producers.
- (d) Mexican coffee producers.

_B_ 14. If we could add all the gains of international trade then subtract all the losses, the net result would be:
- (a) Zero; the gains and losses would cancel out.
- (b) Positive; a net gain for the world and each country.
- (c) Negative; a net loss for the world and each country.
- (d) Positive some years and negative other years.

_____B_____ 15. Protectionism achieves which of the following goals?
- (a) Greater consumption possibilities through greater specialization.
- (b) Protection from microeconomic losses.
- (c) Protection of comparative advantage.
- (d) Protection of absolute advantage.

_____A_____ 16. Tariffs result in:
- (a) Higher employment and output in protected industries than would otherwise be the case.
- (b) Lower domestic prices than those that would prevail in their absence.
- (c) A stimulus to efficient American firms that are not protected.
- (d) A more efficient allocation of resources than would occur in their absence.

_____D_____ 17. As trade restrictions are eliminated, increased imports:
- (a) Lower competition in product markets.
- (b) Leave the composition of the GDP unchanged.
- (c) Redistribute income out of import-using industries.
- (d) Alter resource allocation away from import-competing industries.

_____C_____ 18. Refer to Figure 17.3 in the text. From a consumer's viewpoint, which of the following policies would be least desirable?
- (a) Tariffs on imported goods.
- (b) Quotas on imported goods.
- (c) No trade.
- (d) Free trade.

_____B_____ 19. When the U.S. dollar loses value compared, for example, to the Japanese yen:
- (a) U.S. producers and consumers will lose.
- (b) U.S. auto producers and workers will gain.
- (c) U.S. consumers of Japanese TV sets will gain.
- (d) Japanese tourists to the U.S. will lose.

_____D_____ 20. Refer to the article entitled "Resource Shifts" on page 385 in the text. The information in this article indicates that:
- (a) The U.S. has a comparative advantage in business services.
- (b) Mexico has a comparative advantage in the production of medicine.
- (c) There is a need for adjustment assistance in both countries.
- (d) The article indicates all of the above.

Problems and Applications

Exercise 1

This exercise shows how trade leads to gains by all trading partners through specialization and comparative advantage.

1. Suppose that Japan has 20 laborers in total and that the United States has 40 laborers. Table 17.2 represents the different levels of productivity for the two countries. (*Be careful:* The table tells you that a worker in Japan can produce two TV sets per day *or* ten bicycles per day, *not* two TV sets and ten bicycles!)

Table 17.2. Output per worker-day in the United States and Japan

Country	TV sets (per day)	Bicycles (per day)
Japan	2	10
United States	1	8

Draw the production-possibilities curves for each country in Figure 17.1. Assume constant costs of production.

Figure 17.1

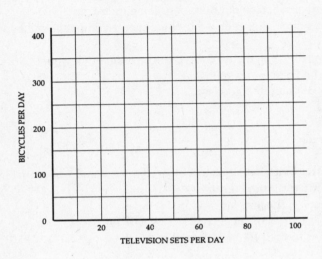

2. Suppose that before trade Japan uses 12 laborers to produce bicycles and 8 laborers to produce television sets; suppose also that in the United States 20 workers produce bicycles and 20 produce television sets. Complete Table 17.3.

Table 17.3. Output produced and consumed without trade

Country	TV sets (per day)	Bicycles (per day)
Japan	_____	_____
United States	_____	_____
Total	_____	_____

3. Before trade, the total output of television sets is _____ ; of bicycles _____ .

4. What is the opportunity cost of one television set in Japan?_____ In the United States?_____

5. What is the opportunity cost of one bicycle in Japan?_____ In the United States?_____

6. If Japan and the United States specialize according to their respective comparative advantages, Japan will produce _____ and the United States will produce_____ . They will do so because the opportunity cost of bicycles in terms of television sets is (lower, higher) in the United States than in Japan, and the opportunity cost of television sets in terms of bicycles is (lower, higher) in Japan than in the United States.

7. After specialization, the total output of television sets is _____ and the total output of bicycles is_____ . (*Hint:* Twenty Japanese produce only TV sets, and 40 Americans produce only bicycles.)

8. This output represents an increase of _____ bicycles and _____television sets over the prespecialization output. (*Hint:* Compare answers to Questions 3 and 7.)

Exercise 2

This exercise will help you understand how the terms of trade are determined. Refer to Exercise 1 for the data.

   If Japan and the United States are to benefit from the increased production, trade must take place. The Japanese will be willing to trade television sets for bicycles as long as they get back more bicycles than they could get in their own country.

1. The terms of trade will be between 1 television set equals _____ bicycles and 1 television set equals _____ bicycles.

2. If the terms of trade were 4 bicycles equals 1 television set:
   (a) Neither country would buy bicycles but both would buy TV sets.
   (b) Neither country would buy TV sets but both would buy bicycles.
   (c) Both countries would buy bicycles and TV sets.
   (d) Neither country would buy TV sets or bicycles.

3. Suppose that the two countries agree that the terms of trade will be 6 bicycles equals 1 television set. Let Japan export 20 television sets per day to the United States. Complete Table 17.4. Assume that Japan produces 40 television sets per day and the United States produces 320 bicycles.

Table 17.4. Consumption combination after trade

Country	TV sets (per day)	Bicycles (per day)
Japan	____	____
United States	____	____
Total	40	320

231

4. As a result of specialization and trade, the United States has the same quantity of television sets and _____ more bicycles per day. (Compare Tables 17.3 and 17.4.)

5. As a result of specialization and trade, Japan has the same number of bicycles and_____ more television sets per day.

Now suppose that at the exchange rate of 6 bicycles to 1 TV set, Japan would like to export 10 TV sets and import 60 bicycles per day. Suppose also that the United States desires to export 90 bicycles and import 15 television sets per day.

6. At these terms of trade there is a (shortage, surplus) of television sets.

7. At these terms of trade there is a (shortage, surplus) of bicycles.

8. Which of the following terms of trade would be more likely to result from this situation?
   (a) 5 bicycles equal 1 television set.
   (b) 6 bicycles equal 1 television set.
   (c) 7 bicycles equal 1 television set.

Exercise 3

Reread the Headline article entitled "Import Quotas" in the text. Then answer the following questions.

1. What sugar grower's argument convinced Congress of the need for a quota on sugar?

2. By how much do domestic sugar prices exceed world sugar prices as a result?

Common Errors

The first statement in each "common error" below is incorrect. Each incorrect statement is followed by a corrected version and an explanation.

1. A country must have an *absolute advantage* in order to gain from trade with another country. WRONG!
   A country must have a *comparative advantage* in order to gain from trade with another country. RIGHT!

   Mutually advantageous trade requires only that the opportunity costs of producing goods differ in the two countries. Another way of stating this is that the production-possibilities curves of the two countries must have different slopes. These two circumstances are indicated in Figure 17.2.

Figure 17.2

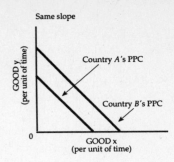 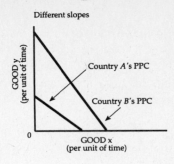

(a) Same slope. Mutually advantageous trade is *not* possible.

(b) Different slopes. Mutually advantageous trade *is* possible.

2. Foreign trade costs a country jobs. WRONG!
Although jobs may be lost, new ones will be created by the opportunities opened up with trade. RIGHT!

When countries specialize and trade according to the law of comparative advantage, some particular workers and firms may be hurt by imports, but the economy as a whole gains by trade. More output per resource input will be attainable. Because the economy is able to reach full employment with trade as well as without trade, there is no reason to assume there will be fewer jobs.

3. A country is well off only as long as it exports more than it imports. WRONG!
Countries may, at times, be well off when they experience a trade surplus: they may also be well off when they have a trade deficit. RIGHT!

Both trade deficits and trade surpluses can be problems if either situation persists for a long period of time. Trade surpluses mean that a country is giving more of its limited, precious resources in trade than it is acquiring from other countries. The currencies of deficit countries tend to depreciate, which means they will be unable to buy as many foreign goods with a unit of currency.

4. Countries tend to enter into trade to get things they cannot produce themselves. WRONG!
Countries very often trade for things they could produce themselves. RIGHT!

Be careful! Countries often trade for things they could produce themselves, because the relative costs of domestic production would be prohibitive. Take baskets as an example. We could certainly produce baskets if we really wanted to. The technique is not difficult to learn and the materials are abundant. But baskets do not lend themselves to machine production, and hand labor is expensive. The cost in terms of goods forgone would be tremendous. (So would the price of the baskets.) We're better off specializing in something like computers, where we have a comparative advantage, and trading for baskets, where we clearly do not have a comparative advantage.

■ ANSWERS ■

Using Key Terms

Across
3. production possibilities
5. consumption possibilities
6. trade surplus
9. exports
11. adjustment assistance
12. trade deficit
13. terms of trade
14. tariff
15. exchange rate

Down
1. equilibrium price
2. voluntary restraint agreement
4. imports
5. comparative advantage
7. opportunity cost
8. absolute advantage
10. quota

True or False

1. F   We both buy and sell large quantities of goods and services, approximately 10 percent of our GDP.
2. T
3. T
4. F   The main reason countries specialize and trade is because total output, income, and living standards are increased.
5. F   It is possible for a country to consume a mix of goods and services beyond its production-possibilities curve when that country specializes and trades.
6. F   A country has a comparative advantage in the production of a good when it can produce the good at a lower opportunity cost than any other country (i.e., it gives up fewer alternative goods and services).
7. T
8. F   There will be losers when a country moves toward freer trade (e.g., import-competing workers and producers). However, the net effect of freer trade is positive for each country and the world.
9. T
10. T

Multiple Choice

1. c	5. b	9. b	13. a, d	17. d
2. c	6. a	10. a	14. b	18. c
3. d	7. c	11. c	15. b	19. b
4. a	8. d	12. d	16. a	20. d

Problems and Applications

Exercise 1

1. **Figure 17.1 Answer**

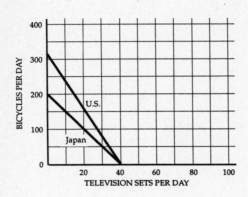

2. **Table 17.3 Answer**

Country	TV sets (per day)	Bicycles (per day)
Japan	16	120
United States	20	160
Total	36	280

3. 36; 280
4. 5 bicycles; 8 bicycles
5. one-fifth of a television set; one-eighth of a television set
6. television sets; bicycles; lower; lower
7. 40; 320
8. 40; 4

Exercise 2

1. 5; 8
2. a

235

3. **Table 17.4 Answer**

Country	TV sets (per day)	Bicycles (per day)
Japan	20	120
United States	20	200
Total	40	320

4. 40
5. 4
6. Shortage. The Japanese wish to export fewer (10) TV sets than Americans want (15).
7. Surplus. The Americans wish to export more (90) bicycles than the Japanese want (60).
8. c

Exercise 3

1. The growers convinced Congress that they deserved protection " ... to ensure a secure supply of sugar in a war."
2. The domestic price of sugar is twice the world price.